Chapter 1: Understanding Market Turbulence

Defining Market Turbulence

Market turbulence refers to periods of significant volatility and uncertainty in financial markets, characterized by rapid price fluctuations and heightened investor anxiety. This phenomenon can be triggered by various factors, including economic events, geopolitical tensions, changes in monetary policy, or unexpected corporate news. Understanding market turbulence is essential for individual investors, as it directly impacts portfolio performance and risk management strategies. The ability to recognize the signs of turbulence allows investors to make informed decisions, potentially mitigating losses and capitalizing on opportunities.

The nature of market turbulence is often influenced by investor psychology. During turbulent periods, fear and greed can drive irrational behavior, leading to panic selling or excessive buying. Behavioral finance helps to explain these reactions, as investors may overreact to negative news or underestimate the impact of positive developments. This emotional response can result in significant market dislocations, creating both risks and opportunities for savvy investors. Recognizing these patterns is crucial for developing a personal risk tolerance framework that aligns with an individual's investment goals and emotional resilience.

Economic indicators play a vital role in defining market turbulence. Key indicators, such as unemployment rates, inflation, and consumer confidence, provide insights into the overall health of the economy. When these indicators signal potential downturns, markets often react with increased volatility. Investors must stay informed about these signals to anticipate periods of turbulence. Utilizing risk assessment tools can further enhance an investor's ability to navigate these turbulent waters, helping to adjust portfolios in response to changing market conditions.

Diversification is a fundamental strategy for managing market turbulence. By spreading investments across various asset classes, sectors, and geographic regions, investors can reduce their exposure to individual stock volatility. During turbulent periods, a well-diversified portfolio may experience less severe fluctuations compared to more concentrated positions. Understanding the interplay between different asset classes and their responses to market changes is essential for effective risk management. Options and futures can also serve as valuable tools for hedging against market turbulence, providing investors with additional layers of protection.

In conclusion, defining market turbulence involves recognizing the interplay between economic indicators, investor psychology, and effective risk management strategies. By equipping themselves with knowledge about market dynamics and utilizing tools for risk assessment, investors can navigate periods of volatility with greater confidence. Developing emotional resilience and a diversified portfolio further empowers individuals to withstand the pressures of turbulent markets. Ultimately, mastering the intricacies of market turbulence is a crucial step in achieving long-term investment success and safeguarding against potential stock market losses.

Historical Context of Market Fluctuations

The historical context of market fluctuations is essential for understanding how past events shape current market dynamics. Major economic events, such as the Great Depression of the 1930s, the dot-com bubble in the late 1990s, and the global financial crisis of 2008, have had profound impacts on investor behavior and market structures. Each of these events revealed vulnerabilities in market systems and prompted regulatory reforms aimed at preventing similar occurrences. By examining the causes and consequences of these fluctuations, investors can better anticipate potential risks and adjust their strategies accordingly.

Behavioral finance plays a crucial role in market fluctuations, as it explores how psychological factors influence investor decisions. Historical market bubbles often illustrate how collective emotions, such as fear and greed, drive irrational behavior. For instance, during the dot-com bubble, many investors overlooked fundamental analysis in favor of exuberance surrounding technology stocks. Understanding these behavioral patterns can help individual investors recognize when market sentiment may be leading to overvaluation or undervaluation, enabling them to make more informed decisions.

Economic indicators are another critical aspect of the historical context of market fluctuations. Indicators such as GDP growth rates, unemployment figures, and inflation rates provide insights into economic health, influencing investor confidence and market performance. Historical analysis of these indicators reveals patterns that can signal potential market movements. By integrating economic data with historical market behavior, investors can develop a more nuanced understanding of how macroeconomic factors contribute to market volatility.

The role of technology in predicting market trends has evolved significantly over time. Advances in data analytics, algorithmic trading, and machine learning have transformed how investors interpret historical data and forecast future movements. Historical fluctuations in market prices can now be analyzed through sophisticated models that account for various risk factors. Understanding these technological advancements allows investors to leverage tools that enhance their risk assessment capabilities and improve their overall market strategies.

Lastly, the historical context of market fluctuations emphasizes the importance of emotional resilience in stock trading. Investors who study past market behavior are better equipped to manage their psychological responses during periods of volatility. Recognizing that fluctuations are a natural part of market cycles can help individuals maintain a long-term perspective, avoiding impulsive decisions driven by short-term market movements. By cultivating emotional resilience and grounding their strategies in historical context, investors can navigate the complexities of the market with greater confidence.

The Importance of Risk Awareness

Risk awareness is a fundamental aspect of successful investing. Understanding the various types of risks involved in the stock market is crucial for individual investors aiming to navigate the complexities of financial markets. Market risk, credit risk, liquidity risk, and operational risk are just a few of the categories that investors must consider. By developing a keen awareness of these risks, investors can make informed decisions, ultimately leading to better financial outcomes. Recognizing that risk is inherent in investing allows individuals to adopt a proactive approach, rather than a reactive one, when facing market fluctuations.

One of the primary reasons risk awareness is vital is that it helps investors identify their personal risk tolerance. Each investor has a unique financial situation and emotional response to market volatility. By understanding one's own capacity for risk, investors can tailor their investment strategies accordingly. This self-awareness not only aids in selecting appropriate investment vehicles but also enhances emotional resilience during market downturns. Those who are aware of their limits are less likely to make impulsive decisions during periods of market stress, which can lead to significant losses.

Furthermore, risk awareness plays a pivotal role in portfolio diversification. A well-diversified portfolio is essential for mitigating risk, as it spreads exposure across various asset classes, sectors, and geographic regions. Investors who are aware of the risks associated with their holdings can identify areas that may be over-concentrated or vulnerable to market shifts. By actively managing their portfolios with a keen eye on risk, investors can better position themselves to weather economic downturns and capitalize on opportunities when they arise.

In addition to personal risk tolerance and diversification, risk awareness is critical for utilizing risk assessment tools effectively. Tools such as Value at Risk (VaR), stress testing, and scenario analysis can provide valuable insights into potential losses under various market conditions. Investors who understand the significance of these tools can better gauge their exposure and make data-driven decisions. Armed with this knowledge, they can implement strategies such as options and futures to hedge against potential losses, further enhancing their risk management capabilities.

Lastly, the importance of risk awareness extends to understanding economic indicators and their impact on stock performance. Investors who stay informed about macroeconomic trends, interest rates, and geopolitical events can anticipate market movements and adjust their strategies accordingly. By being aware of the broader economic landscape, investors can better navigate uncertainties and minimize the impact of adverse events on their portfolios. In summary, cultivating risk awareness is a critical component of mastering market risk, empowering investors to make informed decisions that align with their financial goals and risk profiles.

Chapter 2: Mastering Market Risk

Common Types of Market Risks

Market risk, often referred to as systematic risk, encompasses the potential for financial loss due to factors that affect the entire market or a significant portion of it. Common types of market risks include equity risk, interest rate risk, currency risk, and commodity risk. Each of these risks plays a crucial role in the investment landscape and can significantly impact stock performance, necessitating a comprehensive understanding for effective risk management.

Equity risk arises from market fluctuations that can lead to a decline in stock prices. This type of risk is inherent in owning stocks, as market sentiment, economic conditions, and company performance can all contribute to price volatility. Investors must recognize that while equities can provide substantial returns, they also expose them to the possibility of significant losses. Strategies such as diversification across various sectors and asset classes can help mitigate equity risk, allowing investors to buffer their portfolios against market downturns.

Interest rate risk is primarily associated with fixed-income securities but can also affect stocks. Changes in interest rates can influence borrowing costs, consumer spending, and overall economic growth, which in turn impacts corporate earnings. When interest rates rise, the cost of capital increases, often leading to lower stock valuations. Investors should monitor central bank policies and economic indicators to better anticipate interest rate movements and adjust their portfolios accordingly, potentially incorporating interest rate hedges through derivatives or diversifying into sectors that may benefit from rising rates.

Currency risk is particularly relevant for investors with international exposure. Fluctuations in exchange rates can affect the value of foreign investments, leading to unexpected gains or losses when converted back to the investor's home currency. Understanding the correlation between currency movements and market performance is essential for managing this type of risk. Investors may employ techniques such as currency hedging through options or futures to protect against adverse movements, thereby stabilizing their returns from foreign investments.

Commodity risk is linked to the volatility of commodity prices, which can affect companies involved in production or consumption of these resources. Fluctuations in prices for oil, metals, and agricultural products can have a cascading effect on related industries and overall market performance. Investors should be cognizant of global supply and demand dynamics, geopolitical events, and other factors that can influence commodity prices. Incorporating commodities into a diversified portfolio can serve as a hedge against inflation and provide additional layers of protection against broader market risks.

Understanding these common types of market risks is essential for developing a robust risk management strategy. By recognizing the inherent risks associated with equity, interest rates, currency fluctuations, and commodities, investors can take proactive steps to safeguard their portfolios. Employing a combination of diversification, hedging techniques, and continuous monitoring of market trends will enhance an investor's ability to navigate the complexities of the market, ultimately leading to more informed and resilient investment decisions.

The Impact of Volatility on Investments

Volatility is a fundamental characteristic of financial markets, profoundly influencing investment strategies and outcomes. It refers to the degree of variation in the price of a financial instrument over time, often measured by standard deviation or variance. For investors, understanding volatility is crucial, as it can indicate the level of risk associated with particular assets. High volatility usually suggests greater price swings, which can create both opportunities and challenges. Investors need to recognize that while volatility can lead to substantial gains during upward trends, it can equally result in significant losses during downturns.

The impact of volatility extends beyond mere price fluctuations; it also affects investor behavior and decision-making processes. Behavioral finance highlights how emotions and cognitive biases can distort rational decision-making, particularly in volatile environments. For instance, during periods of high volatility, investors may experience heightened fear or greed, leading to impulsive trading decisions. This can result in panic selling or excessive buying, which further exacerbates market fluctuations. Recognizing these psychological factors is essential for developing a sound investment strategy that mitigates the adverse effects of volatility.

To navigate the challenges presented by volatility, investors should employ comprehensive risk assessment tools. These tools enable individuals to measure and evaluate the risks associated with their portfolios, factoring in the potential for market fluctuations. Common methods include Value at Risk (VaR) and stress testing, which help investors understand their exposure to extreme market conditions. By utilizing these tools, investors can make informed decisions about asset allocation and diversification strategies, ultimately enhancing their ability to withstand market volatility.

Diversification is one of the most effective strategies for managing investment risk in volatile markets. By spreading investments across various asset classes, sectors, and geographic regions, investors can reduce the overall risk of their portfolios. In volatile markets, certain assets may perform poorly while others thrive, allowing a diversified portfolio to weather fluctuations more effectively. Additionally, incorporating alternative investments, such as commodities or real estate, can provide further insulation against market volatility, as these assets often respond differently to economic conditions.

Finally, the integration of technology in market analysis can significantly improve an investor's ability to anticipate and respond to volatility. Advanced algorithms and data analytics can identify patterns and trends, offering insights that may not be immediately apparent through traditional analysis. By leveraging these technological tools, investors can enhance their market predictions and develop more robust risk management strategies. Ultimately, a proactive approach to understanding and managing volatility is essential for achieving long-term investment success, particularly in an ever-changing market landscape.

Developing an Effective Risk Management Mindset

Developing an effective risk management mindset is crucial for investors seeking to navigate the complexities of the stock market. At its core, this mindset involves recognizing that risk is an inherent part of investing, and that understanding and managing this risk can significantly enhance the chances of achieving financial success. An effective risk management approach requires investors to cultivate self-awareness, enabling them to identify their own risk tolerance and emotional responses to market fluctuations. This self-awareness serves as the foundation upon which effective strategies can be built, allowing investors to make informed decisions under pressure.

To foster a robust risk management mindset, investors should prioritize education and continuous learning. Familiarity with various risk assessment tools, such as value-at-risk (VaR) and scenario analysis, empowers individuals to quantify potential losses and understand the implications of different investment strategies. By actively engaging with these tools, investors can develop a clearer picture of the risks associated with their portfolios. Furthermore, staying informed about economic indicators and their impact on market trends is essential in enhancing one's ability to anticipate risks and make proactive adjustments to investment strategies.

Emotional resilience plays a pivotal role in effective risk management. Market volatility can trigger emotional reactions that lead to impulsive decisions, often resulting in significant losses. By cultivating emotional resilience, investors can maintain a level-headed approach even during turbulent market conditions. Techniques such as mindfulness, stress management, and developing a disciplined trading routine can help investors stay focused on their long-term goals rather than succumbing to short-term market movements. This emotional fortitude is essential in adhering to a well-structured risk management plan.

Diversification remains a cornerstone of risk management. By spreading investments across various asset classes, sectors, and geographic regions, investors can mitigate the impact of any single market event on their overall portfolio. This strategy not only reduces risk but also enhances the potential for returns. Investors should periodically reassess their diversification strategies in light of changing market conditions and personal risk tolerances, ensuring that their portfolios remain aligned with their financial objectives and risk appetite.

Finally, leveraging technology can significantly enhance an investor's risk management capabilities. Advanced analytics, machine learning, and algorithmic trading can provide valuable insights into market trends and potential risks. By utilizing these tools, investors can develop more sophisticated strategies for hedging against market downturns, such as using options and futures. Combining technology with a solid risk management mindset enables investors to make data-driven decisions, ultimately leading to more resilient investment portfolios and better outcomes in the face of market uncertainties.

Chapter 3: Behavioral Finance and Market Risk

Psychological Factors Influencing Investment Decisions

Psychological factors play a crucial role in shaping investment decisions, significantly influencing how investors perceive risk and opportunities in the market. Behavioral finance highlights that emotions, biases, and psychological tendencies can lead to irrational decision-making, which often results in suboptimal investing outcomes. Investors may allow fear and greed to dictate their choices, causing them to buy high during market euphoria or sell low in times of panic. Understanding these psychological elements is essential for individuals seeking to master market risk and improve their investment strategies.

One common psychological bias that affects investors is overconfidence. Many individuals tend to overestimate their knowledge and predictive abilities regarding market movements, leading to excessive trading and risk-taking. This overconfidence can result in ignoring critical economic indicators and analytical tools necessary for informed decision-making. Investors must cultivate a realistic assessment of their capabilities and recognize the inherent uncertainties of the market to avoid the pitfalls of overconfidence, thereby enhancing their risk management strategies.

Another significant psychological factor is loss aversion, which is the tendency to prefer avoiding losses rather than acquiring equivalent gains. Research shows that the emotional distress associated with losses is more intense than the pleasure derived from gains of the same magnitude. This aversion can prevent investors from holding onto underperforming assets long enough for a potential recovery or from diversifying their portfolios effectively. By acknowledging loss aversion, investors can develop a more balanced approach to risk assessment and decision-making, allowing them to stay focused on long-term objectives rather than immediate emotional responses.

Moreover, the concept of herd behavior illustrates how social dynamics can influence individual investment choices. Investors often look to the actions of their peers or market trends, which can lead to collective irrationality. This behavior can result in asset bubbles or market crashes, as decisions based on group sentiment override personal analysis and sound risk management principles. To counteract herd behavior, investors must cultivate independent thinking and rely on thorough research and data analysis to guide their investment strategies, fostering resilience against market volatility.

Finally, emotional resilience is a critical skill for navigating the psychological challenges of investing. The ability to manage one's emotions, particularly during periods of market stress, can significantly impact decision-making processes. Developing emotional resilience involves practicing mindfulness, maintaining a disciplined investment strategy, and setting clear goals that align with one's risk tolerance. By fostering resilience, investors can mitigate the adverse effects of psychological factors, making more rational and informed decisions that align with their long-term financial objectives.

Recognizing Cognitive Biases

Cognitive biases significantly influence the decision-making processes of investors, often leading them to make irrational choices that can result in substantial market losses. Recognizing these biases is a crucial first step in mastering market risk. Investors frequently fall prey to confirmation bias, where they favor information that supports their existing beliefs while disregarding contrary evidence. This can create a distorted view of market conditions, causing them to hold onto losing investments longer than they should or to overlook promising opportunities that do not fit their preconceived notions.

Another prevalent cognitive bias is overconfidence, which can lead investors to overestimate their knowledge or predictive capabilities.

This bias often manifests in excessive trading or concentration in a limited number of stocks, as investors believe they can outperform the market based on their research or intuition. Such overestimation can result in significant losses, particularly in volatile markets where uncertainty is high. Recognizing one's own overconfidence is essential for developing a more disciplined and rational investment strategy.

Loss aversion is yet another cognitive bias that can distort an investor's judgment. Research shows that individuals tend to prefer avoiding losses over acquiring equivalent gains, which can lead to an overly conservative investment approach. Investors may hold onto losing stocks in the hope of recouping their losses instead of reallocating capital to more promising opportunities. Acknowledging this bias can help investors cultivate a more balanced perspective, enabling them to make decisions based on potential gains rather than the fear of losing money.

Herding behavior is also a significant cognitive bias that can impact market dynamics. Investors often follow the crowd, buying or selling based on what others are doing rather than their own analysis. This can exacerbate market trends, leading to asset bubbles or crashes. Recognizing the tendency to conform to group behavior can empower individual investors to make more independent and informed choices, potentially safeguarding them from the pitfalls of market hysteria.

Finally, the effect of emotional states on investment decisions cannot be underestimated. Fear and greed are powerful motivators that can cloud judgment and lead to impulsive actions. Investors may react emotionally to market fluctuations, leading to panic selling in downturns or euphoric buying during bull markets. Developing emotional resilience and employing strategies to mitigate these feelings can enhance an investor's ability to navigate market risks effectively. By recognizing and addressing cognitive biases, investors can cultivate a more rational approach to their investment strategies, ultimately reducing the likelihood of substantial losses in the stock market.

Strategies to Mitigate Emotional Decision-Making

Emotional decision-making can significantly undermine investment strategies, leading to substantial market losses. To mitigate the effects of emotions on trading decisions, investors can implement several practical strategies. One effective approach is to establish a well-defined investment plan that outlines clear goals, risk tolerance, and asset allocation. By adhering to a structured plan, investors can reduce the likelihood of making impulsive decisions driven by fear or greed. This plan should be revisited periodically to ensure it remains aligned with changing market conditions and personal circumstances, fostering a disciplined investment mindset.

Another essential strategy is to utilize data-driven tools and analytics to guide investment choices. Behavioral finance highlights that emotions can cloud judgment, making it crucial for investors to rely on objective data rather than subjective feelings. By employing risk assessment tools, such as technical analysis or fundamental valuation metrics, investors can make informed decisions based on market trends and economic indicators. This reliance on empirical data helps counteract emotional biases and reinforces a rational approach to investing.

Incorporating mindfulness and emotional awareness into the trading process can also be beneficial. Practicing mindfulness techniques allows investors to recognize their emotional triggers and respond more thoughtfully rather than reactively. Techniques such as meditation, journaling, or even regular reflection on trading experiences can enhance emotional resilience. By fostering a greater understanding of their emotional landscape, investors can better navigate the psychological challenges of stock trading and maintain focus on their long-term objectives.

Diversification serves as another crucial strategy for mitigating emotional decision-making. By spreading investments across various asset classes, sectors, and geographical regions, investors can reduce the impact of market volatility on their portfolios. This approach not only lowers risk but can also alleviate the emotional stress associated with individual stock fluctuations. When markets experience downturns, a diversified portfolio is less likely to incur drastic losses, allowing investors to remain calm and stick to their strategies without succumbing to panic selling.

Finally, ongoing education about market dynamics and risk management techniques is vital for maintaining a rational investment approach. Investors should seek to enhance their understanding of economic indicators, market trends, and the implications of global events on their portfolios. Continuous learning empowers investors to make well-informed decisions and reinforces confidence in their strategies. By combining education with practical tools and emotional awareness, investors can create a robust framework for navigating the complexities of the stock market while minimizing the adverse effects of emotional decision-making.

Chapter 4: Risk Assessment Tools for Individual Investors

Key Metrics for Evaluating Investment Risk

Key metrics for evaluating investment risk serve as essential tools for investors seeking to navigate the complexities of the stock market. Understanding these metrics allows individuals to assess potential losses, measure volatility, and make informed decisions that align with their investment strategies. Key metrics such as standard deviation, beta, value at risk (VaR), and Sharpe ratio provide a quantitative foundation for evaluating the risk associated with various investments. By mastering these metrics, investors can not only avoid significant losses but also enhance their overall market performance.

Standard deviation is a critical metric that measures the dispersion of an asset's returns around its mean. A higher standard deviation indicates greater volatility, which implies a higher level of risk. For investors, understanding standard deviation is crucial in determining how much an investment's returns can vary over time. This metric allows them to compare the risk profiles of different assets, aiding in the selection of investments that align with their risk tolerance. By incorporating standard deviation into their evaluation process, investors can make more informed decisions about which stocks to include in their portfolios.

Beta is another vital metric that assesses the sensitivity of an investment's returns to market movements. A beta greater than one suggests that the asset is more volatile than the overall market, while a beta less than one indicates lower volatility. By analyzing beta, investors can gauge how much risk they are taking on relative to the market. This metric is particularly useful for constructing diversified portfolios, as it helps investors balance their exposure to market fluctuations. Understanding beta empowers investors to make strategic choices that can mitigate risk and enhance their portfolio's resilience.

Value at risk (VaR) offers a probabilistic estimate of the potential loss an investor might face over a specified time frame, given normal market conditions. VaR is particularly useful for risk management, as it quantifies the worst-case scenario and provides a clear benchmark for assessing risk exposure. Investors can use VaR to set limits on potential losses, thereby establishing a framework for risk management that aligns with their financial goals. By incorporating VaR into their investment strategy, individuals can make more informed decisions about their asset allocation and risk tolerance.

The Sharpe ratio is a key performance metric that evaluates an investment's return relative to its risk. By comparing the excess return of an investment to its standard deviation, the Sharpe ratio enables investors to assess the efficiency of their portfolios. A higher Sharpe ratio signifies a more favorable risk-return profile, indicating that an investment delivers better returns for each unit of risk taken. This metric is invaluable for investors seeking to optimize their portfolios and achieve their financial objectives. By understanding and utilizing these key metrics, investors can enhance their ability to manage market risk effectively and make informed investment decisions that lead to long-term success.

Utilizing Risk Assessment Software

Utilizing risk assessment software is a critical component for investors seeking to navigate the complexities of the stock market effectively. This technology enables individual investors to quantify their exposure to various risks, including market volatility, economic shifts, and behavioral biases. By employing sophisticated algorithms and data analytics, risk assessment software provides insights that can help users make informed decisions, ultimately enhancing their ability to avoid significant losses. For those aiming to master market risk, understanding how to leverage these tools is essential for both strategic planning and real-time decision-making.

The first step in utilizing risk assessment software is to identify the specific needs and objectives of the investor. Different tools may cater to various aspects of risk management, from portfolio analysis and stress testing to scenario simulation and performance tracking. By aligning the software's capabilities with personal investment goals and risk tolerance, investors can ensure they are using the most relevant features to their advantage. This tailored approach not only increases the effectiveness of the analysis but also fosters a deeper understanding of how different risks can impact overall portfolio performance.

Another significant advantage of risk assessment software is its ability to incorporate real-time data and economic indicators. Investors can access up-to-date information on market trends, geopolitical events, and economic forecasts, allowing them to adjust their strategies promptly. This dynamic capability is particularly vital in a fast-paced market where conditions can change rapidly. Furthermore, the integration of behavioral finance principles within the software helps investors recognize cognitive biases that may affect their decision-making processes, enabling them to mitigate emotional responses to market fluctuations.

In addition to enhancing individual decision-making, risk assessment software can facilitate better communication among stakeholders. For those managing portfolios on behalf of clients or within larger investment firms, the ability to generate comprehensive risk reports can improve transparency and trust. These reports not only outline potential risks but also provide actionable insights based on data-driven analyses. By presenting clear and concise information, investors can effectively articulate their strategies and justify their decisions, reinforcing their credibility in the eyes of clients or partners.

Finally, the implementation of risk assessment software encourages a proactive approach to investment management. Rather than reacting to market changes after they occur, investors can anticipate potential risks and develop contingency plans. This forward-thinking mindset is essential for successful risk management, particularly in volatile markets. By continuously monitoring risk exposure and adjusting their strategies based on analytical insights, investors can build resilience into their portfolios, ultimately leading to more sustainable investment practices and greater long-term success in the stock market.

Creating a Personalized Risk Assessment Plan

Creating a personalized risk assessment plan is a crucial step for any investor looking to navigate the complexities of the stock market. This plan serves as a tailored roadmap that aligns an investor's financial goals, risk tolerance, and investment strategies with their individual circumstances. By understanding the specific risks associated with their investments, investors can make informed decisions that minimize potential losses while maximizing opportunities for growth. A personalized risk assessment plan should consider various factors, including market volatility, economic conditions, and personal financial situations.

The first step in developing a personalized risk assessment plan is to evaluate individual risk tolerance. This involves an honest appraisal of one's ability to handle the ups and downs of the market. Risk tolerance is not static; it can be influenced by factors such as age, investment experience, financial goals, and psychological disposition towards risk. Investors should utilize questionnaires and tools designed to gauge their risk appetite, which can help them understand how much volatility they are willing to accept in pursuit of higher returns.

Following the assessment of risk tolerance, the next phase is to identify and analyze potential risks associated with various investment options. This includes understanding market risks, credit risks, liquidity risks, and operational risks that can affect investment portfolios. Investors should employ risk assessment tools, such as Value at Risk (VaR) and stress testing, to quantify potential losses under different market conditions. This analysis not only highlights vulnerabilities but also helps in crafting strategies to mitigate those risks through diversification and asset allocation.

Incorporating economic indicators into the risk assessment plan is vital for making informed decisions. Investors should monitor key economic metrics such as interest rates, inflation rates, and employment figures, as these indicators can significantly impact market performance. Understanding how these factors correlate with specific investments allows investors to adjust their portfolios proactively, ensuring alignment with broader economic trends. This foresight can help in navigating market downturns and identifying opportune moments for investment.

Lastly, emotional resilience plays a pivotal role in the success of a personalized risk assessment plan. Market fluctuations can evoke strong emotional responses, leading to impulsive decisions that deviate from an investor's original strategy. Developing emotional resilience involves cultivating a mindset that focuses on long-term goals rather than short-term market movements. By integrating psychological strategies, such as mindfulness and self-reflection, investors can maintain discipline in their investment approach. A well-rounded risk assessment plan not only addresses financial metrics but also incorporates emotional and psychological factors, ultimately leading to more successful investment outcomes.

Chapter 5: Strategies for Diversifying Stock Portfolios

The Importance of Diversification

Diversification is a fundamental principle in investment strategy that seeks to mitigate risk and enhance portfolio performance. By spreading investments across various asset classes, sectors, and geographical regions, investors can reduce their exposure to any single economic event or market downturn. This approach is rooted in the understanding that different assets often react differently to market conditions. For instance, while stocks may decline during economic recessions, bonds or commodities might perform better, providing a buffer against losses. Thus, a well-diversified portfolio can offer more stable returns over time, making it a cornerstone of effective risk management.

Behavioral finance highlights the psychological biases that can influence investor decision-making. Many investors fall prey to the temptation of concentrating their investments in familiar stocks or sectors, often leading to significant risk exposure. Diversification counters this tendency by encouraging a broader perspective and a more disciplined investment approach. By diversifying, investors can avoid the pitfalls of overconfidence and herd behavior, which can lead to poor investment choices. This practice fosters a more rational investment strategy, allowing individuals to focus on long-term goals rather than short-term market fluctuations.

Furthermore, diversification is particularly critical in the context of market volatility. Economic indicators such as interest rates, inflation, and geopolitical events can create unpredictable market environments. An investor with a concentrated portfolio may experience sharp declines in value during turbulent times, while a diversified portfolio can help cushion the impact. For example, asset classes such as real estate or international stocks may respond differently to domestic economic shifts, serving as a stabilizing force. This resilience is vital for investors who are planning for long-term objectives, such as retirement, where maintaining capital is essential.

Incorporating diversification into an investment strategy also involves the use of various risk assessment tools. Individual investors can utilize analytics and market trend indicators to identify potential risks associated with specific assets. By assessing the correlation between different investments, they can construct a portfolio designed to minimize risk while aiming for optimal returns. Technology plays a significant role in this process, allowing investors to backtest strategies and model potential outcomes based on historical data. This informed approach to diversification can significantly enhance an investor's ability to manage market risk.

Ultimately, the importance of diversification extends beyond mere risk mitigation; it is an essential component of an effective investment strategy. It encourages a disciplined approach, reduces the impact of market volatility, and allows investors to better navigate the complexities of the financial landscape. By understanding and implementing diversification, individuals can build resilient portfolios that align with their personal risk tolerance and investment objectives, paving the way for financial stability and growth in the long run.

Asset Allocation Techniques

Asset allocation techniques are essential strategies that investors utilize to manage risk and optimize returns within their portfolios. By distributing investments across various asset classes, such as stocks, bonds, real estate, and commodities, investors can mitigate the impact of market volatility and reduce the likelihood of significant losses. A well-planned asset allocation strategy takes into account individual risk tolerance, investment goals, and time horizons, ensuring a balanced approach to capital growth and protection against adverse market movements.

One common technique employed in asset allocation is strategic asset allocation, which involves setting long-term targets for the proportion of different asset classes in a portfolio. This approach is grounded in modern portfolio theory, which posits that a diversified portfolio can enhance returns while minimizing risk. By periodically rebalancing the portfolio to align with these targets, investors can take advantage of market fluctuations, buying low and selling high to maintain their desired risk profile. This discipline is particularly important as it helps investors avoid emotional decision-making during turbulent market conditions.

Another technique is tactical asset allocation, which allows for short-term adjustments based on market conditions and economic indicators. This strategy involves actively shifting the proportion of assets in response to market trends, economic forecasts, or shifts in investor sentiment. While tactical allocation can potentially lead to higher returns by capitalizing on market opportunities, it also introduces the risk of making poor timing decisions. Therefore, investors must employ careful analysis and an understanding of market dynamics to effectively implement this strategy without succumbing to emotional biases.

Dynamic asset allocation is a more flexible approach that adjusts the allocation to different asset classes based on changing market conditions and individual circumstances. This technique recognizes that risk tolerance may evolve over time, influenced by factors such as age, financial status, or market environment. Investors who adopt dynamic asset allocation must remain vigilant and responsive, making informed adjustments to their portfolios to align with their current risk tolerance and investment objectives. This adaptability can provide a significant advantage in navigating market uncertainties while maintaining a focus on long-term goals.

Lastly, risk parity is an innovative technique that emphasizes equal risk contribution from all asset classes within a portfolio rather than equal capital allocation. This method aims to balance the volatility and risk of various assets, leading to a more stable overall portfolio performance. By allocating capital based on the risk profile of each asset class, investors can potentially enhance returns while reducing the likelihood of large losses. Understanding and implementing risk parity requires a solid grasp of the correlations between asset classes and their historical performance, making it a sophisticated strategy suitable for more experienced investors.

Evaluating Sector and Geographic Diversification

Evaluating sector and geographic diversification is essential for constructing a resilient investment portfolio. Sector diversification involves spreading investments across various industries to mitigate the risk that any single sector underperforms. Different sectors often react differently to economic changes, regulatory shifts, and market trends. For instance, during economic downturns, defensive sectors such as utilities and consumer staples may perform better than cyclical sectors like technology and luxury goods. Understanding these dynamics allows investors to position their portfolios to weather market fluctuations and reduce the overall risk of significant losses.

Geographic diversification, on the other hand, entails spreading investments across different countries and regions. This strategy takes into account the varying economic conditions, political climates, and currency risks associated with different markets. For example, investing in emerging markets can provide growth opportunities that are not available in more mature economies. However, these markets may also present higher volatility and risk. An effective approach to geographic diversification helps investors capture growth in diverse economic environments while minimizing the potential impact of localized downturns.

When assessing sector and geographic diversification, investors should utilize a variety of risk assessment tools. These tools can include correlation analysis, which evaluates how different sectors and geographic markets move in relation to one another. By understanding these correlations, investors can make informed decisions about how to allocate their capital effectively.

Additionally, employing economic indicators, such as GDP growth rates, inflation trends, and employment statistics, can provide valuable insights into which sectors and regions may offer the best opportunities for growth or protection against risk.

Emotional resilience plays a crucial role in the evaluation of diversification strategies. Investors often face the temptation to make impulsive decisions based on short-term market movements. It is essential to remain committed to a well-thought-out diversification plan, even when market conditions are challenging. Developing a personal risk tolerance framework can aid investors in maintaining focus on their long-term goals while managing the emotional highs and lows that come with investing. This framework should include predefined criteria for sector and geographic allocation, ensuring that investors stay aligned with their overall risk management strategy.

In conclusion, evaluating sector and geographic diversification is a critical aspect of effective market risk management. By understanding the importance of spreading investments across various industries and regions, investors can reduce their exposure to volatility and enhance their portfolio's resilience. Utilizing risk assessment tools, staying emotionally balanced, and adhering to a personal risk tolerance framework are essential steps in mastering market risk. Ultimately, a well-diversified portfolio can lead to more stable returns and a greater likelihood of achieving long-term investment success.

Chapter 6: Understanding Economic Indicators and Their Impact on Stocks

Key Economic Indicators to Monitor

Understanding key economic indicators is essential for investors looking to navigate the complexities of the stock market effectively. These indicators provide valuable insights into the overall health of the economy and can significantly influence market trends. By examining these metrics, investors can make informed decisions, adjust their strategies, and potentially avoid significant losses. Key economic indicators include metrics such as Gross Domestic Product (GDP), unemployment rates, inflation rates, and consumer confidence indexes, each serving a unique purpose in assessing economic conditions.

Gross Domestic Product (GDP) is one of the most critical indicators, representing the total value of all goods and services produced over a specific time period. A growing GDP typically signals a healthy economy, which can lead to increased consumer spending and business investment. Conversely, a declining GDP may indicate an economic slowdown, prompting investors to reassess their positions and strategies. Monitoring GDP growth rates can help investors anticipate market movements and adjust their portfolios accordingly, thus mitigating potential risks.

Unemployment rates are another vital economic indicator. High unemployment often correlates with reduced consumer spending, as fewer people have disposable income to spend on goods and services. This decline can negatively impact corporate earnings and, consequently, stock prices. Conversely, low unemployment rates can suggest a strong economy where businesses thrive and job creation is robust. By tracking unemployment trends, investors can gauge market conditions and consumer confidence, allowing them to make proactive investment choices.

Inflation rates also play a crucial role in the investment landscape. Moderate inflation can indicate a growing economy, but excessive inflation may erode purchasing power and lead to increased interest rates. Investors must be aware of inflation trends to understand how they affect corporate profits and stock valuations. An effective strategy involves monitoring inflation indicators, such as the Consumer Price Index (CPI), to anticipate potential shifts in monetary policy and market dynamics.

Lastly, the Consumer Confidence Index (CCI) is a powerful indicator of how optimistic or pessimistic consumers feel about the economy. High consumer confidence typically correlates with increased spending, which can boost economic growth and stock performance. Conversely, declining consumer confidence can signal potential economic challenges ahead. By keeping an eye on the CCI, investors can gauge market sentiment and make informed decisions about their investment strategies, ultimately enhancing their ability to manage risks effectively. Understanding these key economic indicators is crucial for any investor aiming to master market risk and achieve long-term success in the stock market.

Analyzing the Relationship Between Economic Data and Stock Performance

Understanding the intricate relationship between economic data and stock performance is crucial for investors aiming to navigate market fluctuations effectively. Economic indicators serve as vital signals that can influence investor sentiment and market behavior. Metrics such as Gross Domestic Product (GDP), unemployment rates, inflation, and consumer confidence are essential in assessing the overall health of an economy. These indicators often lead to shifts in market expectations, impacting stock prices and investment strategies. Investors must analyze these data points not only in isolation but also in conjunction with other factors that may sway market dynamics.

The correlation between economic data and stock performance is often evident in market reactions to new information. For instance, a rise in unemployment rates can lead to a decline in consumer spending, prompting a bearish outlook for companies reliant on consumer discretionary spending. Conversely, positive economic data, such as a surge in GDP growth, can inspire bullish sentiment, driving stock prices upward. Understanding these patterns allows investors to make informed decisions about buying or selling stocks based on anticipated market movements resulting from economic shifts.

Behavioral finance plays a significant role in how investors perceive and react to economic data. Cognitive biases, such as overconfidence and loss aversion, can skew decision-making processes, leading investors to misinterpret economic signals. For example, when facing negative economic indicators, investors might panic and sell their holdings prematurely, potentially locking in losses. Conversely, during periods of positive economic news, they may become overly optimistic, forgetting the inherent risks involved. A clear understanding of these psychological factors is essential for developing a balanced approach to stock trading, mitigating emotional responses to market changes.

Risk assessment tools are invaluable in analyzing the potential impact of economic data on stock performance. Tools such as scenario analysis and stress testing can help investors gauge how various economic conditions might affect their portfolios. By simulating different economic scenarios, investors can better understand potential risks and returns, allowing for the development of a more resilient investment strategy. These assessments provide a framework for evaluating how changing economic conditions may necessitate adjustments in stock allocations or diversification strategies.

Incorporating economic indicators into investment strategies can enhance portfolio resilience. Diversifying across sectors that respond differently to economic data can minimize risks associated with adverse market movements. For instance, defensive stocks, which typically perform well during economic downturns, can provide stability when broader market conditions are unfavorable. By staying informed about economic trends and their potential implications for stock performance, investors can better position themselves to weather market volatility, ensuring a more robust and adaptable investment approach.

Strategies for Adjusting Investment Based on Economic Trends

Understanding economic trends is essential for investors looking to adjust their investment strategies effectively. Economic indicators such as GDP growth rates, unemployment figures, inflation, and consumer confidence provide valuable insights into the overall health of the economy. By closely monitoring these indicators, investors can anticipate market movements and make informed decisions about when to enter or exit specific positions. For instance, a rising GDP may indicate a robust economy, prompting investors to increase their equity exposure, while high inflation rates could lead them to consider more defensive assets like bonds or commodities.

Behavioral finance plays a critical role in how investors react to economic trends. Psychological biases, such as overconfidence and loss aversion, can cloud judgment and lead to poor decision-making. Recognizing these biases allows investors to develop strategies that counteract their emotional impulses. For instance, setting predefined rules for asset allocation based on economic indicators can help mitigate the impact of irrational behavior. This structured approach promotes discipline and encourages investors to stick to their strategies, even in volatile market conditions.

Diversification remains a cornerstone strategy for managing risk in response to economic changes. By spreading investments across various asset classes, sectors, and geographic regions, investors can reduce their exposure to any single economic downturn. For example, during periods of economic contraction, sectors like consumer staples and utilities may outperform more cyclical sectors like technology and discretionary goods. Investors should continuously assess their portfolios to ensure they are adequately diversified and aligned with prevailing economic trends, allowing them to buffer against market volatility.

Utilizing risk assessment tools can further enhance an investor's ability to adjust their strategies based on economic trends. Tools such as scenario analysis, stress testing, and value-at-risk (VaR) models help quantify potential losses and assess the impact of different economic conditions on a portfolio. By employing these tools, investors can make data-driven decisions, identifying areas of vulnerability and opportunity. Additionally, technology plays a pivotal role in gathering and analyzing economic data, enabling investors to stay ahead of trends and adjust their strategies proactively.

Finally, developing emotional resilience is crucial for navigating the complexities of market risk. Investors must cultivate the ability to remain calm and rational during periods of uncertainty and stress. This resilience can be fostered through practices such as mindfulness and continuous education about market dynamics. By maintaining a balanced perspective and focusing on long-term goals, investors can better manage their responses to economic fluctuations, leading to more effective investment strategies that align with their risk tolerance and financial objectives.

Chapter 7: Using Options and Futures to Hedge Market Risk

Introduction to Derivatives

Derivatives are financial instruments whose value is derived from the performance of an underlying asset, index, or rate. They include a variety of contracts, such as options, futures, and swaps, which can serve multiple purposes in the financial markets. Understanding derivatives is crucial for investors interested in managing market risk effectively. They provide opportunities for hedging against losses, speculating on future price movements, and enhancing portfolio performance. As such, derivatives can be powerful tools for both individual investors and institutional players seeking to navigate the complexities of the stock market.

One of the primary functions of derivatives is hedging, which involves taking a position in a derivative to offset potential losses in another investment. For example, an investor holding a stock might purchase put options to protect against a decline in the stock's price. This strategic use of derivatives allows investors to mitigate their exposure to market volatility. In the context of risk management, derivatives can be an essential part of a broader strategy, offering a way to control risk while still participating in potential market gains.

In addition to hedging, derivatives can also be used for speculation. Traders may use futures contracts to bet on the direction of asset prices, seeking to profit from short-term market movements. While speculative trading can lead to significant gains, it also carries substantial risks. Understanding the mechanics of derivatives is vital for investors who wish to engage in speculation, as it enables them to make informed decisions and manage their risk exposure effectively.

Another important aspect of derivatives is their role in enhancing portfolio diversification. By incorporating derivatives into an investment strategy, investors can create a more balanced portfolio that can withstand market fluctuations. For instance, using options can provide additional income through premium collection while maintaining exposure to underlying assets. This diversification can be particularly beneficial during periods of market stress, where traditional asset classes may become highly correlated.

Finally, the use of technology has significantly transformed the landscape of derivatives trading and risk management. Advanced algorithms, data analytics, and real-time market monitoring allow investors to make more informed decisions regarding their derivative positions. Understanding how technology impacts the pricing and trading of derivatives is essential for modern investors. As financial markets continue to evolve, mastering the use of derivatives will be increasingly important for those seeking to effectively manage risk and enhance their investment strategies.

Basic Strategies for Options and Futures

Options and futures are powerful financial instruments that can be used to manage risk and enhance investment strategies. Understanding these derivatives is crucial for investors looking to protect their portfolios against market volatility. Basic strategies for options and futures involve a combination of hedging, speculation, and income generation, each serving distinct purposes within a comprehensive investment approach. By grasping these strategies, investors can better navigate the complexities of market risk and position themselves for potential gains while mitigating losses.

One fundamental strategy in options trading is hedging, which involves using options to offset potential losses in an underlying asset. For instance, purchasing a put option grants the investor the right to sell the asset at a predetermined price, offering protection against declines. This approach is particularly useful during market downturns, as it allows investors to maintain ownership of their stocks while having a safety net in place. By employing this strategy, investors can preserve capital and reduce the emotional impact of market fluctuations.

Futures contracts, on the other hand, are agreements to buy or sell an asset at a specified future date and price. They can be used for speculation, allowing investors to bet on the direction of market prices. For example, if an investor anticipates a rise in oil prices, they could take a long position in crude oil futures. This potential for profit comes with significant risk, as futures can lead to substantial losses if market movements go against the investor's position. Understanding the inherent risks associated with futures is essential for developing a balanced approach to market participation.

Another strategy involves the use of covered calls, where an investor holds a long position in an asset and sells call options on that same asset. This technique generates income through premiums received from selling the call options while still allowing for potential appreciation of the underlying asset. Covered calls can be an effective way to enhance returns in a flat or mildly bullish market while providing some downside protection. As with any strategy, investors should assess their risk tolerance and market outlook before implementing covered calls.

Finally, combining options and futures strategies with robust risk assessment tools is vital for individual investors. Employing techniques such as value-at-risk (VaR) and stress testing can provide insights into potential losses under various market scenarios. By integrating these analytical tools with options and futures strategies, investors can make informed decisions that align with their financial goals and risk tolerance. Overall, mastering these basic strategies equips investors with the knowledge to navigate market risks effectively and pursue their investment objectives with confidence.

Risk Management Benefits of Hedging

Hedging is a critical component of risk management that allows investors to protect their portfolios from adverse market movements.

By using financial instruments such as options and futures, investors can create strategies that offset potential losses in their primary investments. This proactive approach is particularly beneficial in volatile markets, where unexpected price swings can significantly impact portfolio performance. Through effective hedging techniques, investors can manage their risk exposure while maintaining the potential for returns.

One of the primary benefits of hedging is the ability to stabilize returns. When investors hedge, they essentially create a safety net that minimizes the impact of unfavorable price movements. This stability is crucial for individual investors who may rely on their portfolios for retirement or other long-term financial goals. By reducing volatility, hedging can enable a more predictable investment outcome, allowing investors to adhere to their financial plans without the stress of drastic market fluctuations.

Moreover, hedging can enhance an investor's emotional resilience. The psychological strain of watching portfolio values decline can lead to irrational decision-making, such as panic selling or impulsive buying. By implementing hedging strategies, investors can alleviate some of this emotional burden, knowing they have taken steps to protect their investments. This peace of mind can lead to better decision-making and a more disciplined approach to investing, ultimately contributing to long-term financial success.

Additionally, hedging plays a vital role in risk assessment and portfolio diversification. It allows investors to quantify their risk exposure and adjust their strategies accordingly. By incorporating hedging into their investment plans, individuals can better align their portfolios with their personal risk tolerance frameworks. This alignment is essential for maintaining a diversified portfolio, as it ensures that all investments work together to achieve the desired risk-return profile.

Lastly, the benefits of hedging extend to the overall market as well. When investors utilize hedging strategies, they contribute to market efficiency by providing liquidity and fostering price discovery. This dynamic can lead to a healthier investment environment, where assets are more accurately valued based on their underlying fundamentals. As investors become more adept at using hedging techniques, they not only protect their own interests but also contribute to a more resilient and stable market overall.

Chapter 8: Emotional Resilience in Stock Trading

The Role of Emotions in Trading

Emotions play a critical role in trading, often influencing decision-making processes and market outcomes. Traders are not just rational actors; they are individuals driven by a complex interplay of feelings such as fear, greed, hope, and anxiety. These emotions can lead to irrational behaviors, which may result in significant financial losses. For example, during market downturns, fear can cause investors to panic-sell their holdings at a loss, while during bullish trends, greed can lead to overexposure to riskier assets. Understanding how emotions impact trading decisions is essential for mastering market risk and developing effective strategies for long-term success.

Fear is one of the most potent emotions in trading, often manifesting as a response to market volatility or negative news. When traders encounter sudden market drops, fear may compel them to liquidate positions hastily, potentially locking in losses. This emotional reaction can be exacerbated by the herd mentality, where individuals follow the actions of others rather than relying on their analytical judgment. Recognizing fear as a natural response can help traders implement strategies to mitigate its influence, such as setting predefined stop-loss orders or maintaining a diversified portfolio to cushion against market shocks.

Conversely, greed can lead to overconfidence, resulting in poor investment choices. Traders may become overly optimistic during periods of rising stock prices, leading to excessive risk-taking and underestimating potential downsides. This emotional high can cloud judgment, causing individuals to ignore critical risk assessment tools and economic indicators that are vital for informed decision-making. To counteract the effects of greed, traders should cultivate a disciplined approach to investing, incorporating systematic strategies that emphasize risk management and adherence to a personal risk tolerance framework.

Hope also plays a significant role in trading behavior. Many traders hold onto losing positions, hoping for a market reversal that may never come. This emotional attachment can lead to a failure to cut losses and reallocate resources more effectively. Developing emotional resilience involves acknowledging these tendencies and establishing a rational decision-making process. Traders can benefit from regular self-reflection and employing techniques such as journaling to track emotional responses and trading outcomes, ultimately fostering a mindset that prioritizes long-term goals over short-term emotional reactions.

In conclusion, understanding the role of emotions in trading is crucial for effective market risk management. By recognizing how fear, greed, and hope influence trading behavior, investors can develop strategies to mitigate their impact. Incorporating emotional awareness into trading practices not only enhances decision-making but also supports the development of a more robust and resilient investment strategy. As traders strive to master market risk, cultivating emotional intelligence becomes an integral component of their overall approach to investing.

Building Emotional Strength

Building emotional strength is crucial for investors seeking to navigate the volatile landscape of the stock market. Emotional resilience allows individuals to maintain composure during market fluctuations, make rational decisions, and avoid impulsive actions driven by fear or greed. Understanding the psychological aspects of trading can significantly enhance an investor's ability to manage risk effectively. By cultivating emotional strength, investors can better adhere to their strategies, remain focused on long-term goals, and ultimately reduce the likelihood of incurring significant losses.

One key aspect of building emotional strength is the recognition of one's emotional triggers. Investors often experience heightened emotions, such as anxiety during market downturns or overexcitement during rallies. By identifying these triggers, investors can develop strategies to cope with them, such as mindfulness techniques or structured decision-making processes. This self-awareness enables them to respond to market events with a level head, rather than reacting impulsively based on short-term emotions. Incorporating regular self-assessment into an investment routine can help reinforce this awareness and promote a disciplined approach to trading.

Another important factor in emotional strength is the cultivation of a supportive network. Engaging with fellow investors, participating in discussion groups, or seeking mentorship can provide valuable perspectives and reassurance. Sharing experiences and strategies with others can help mitigate feelings of isolation and uncertainty that often accompany market volatility. Moreover, a supportive community can serve as a source of encouragement during challenging times, reminding investors of their long-term objectives and reinforcing their commitment to sound investment principles.

Setting realistic expectations is also vital in the journey toward emotional resilience. Investors should understand that losses are an inherent part of the market and that no strategy is foolproof. By establishing achievable goals and accepting the possibility of setbacks, investors can buffer themselves against emotional distress. This mindset encourages a focus on the bigger picture, allowing individuals to view short-term fluctuations as mere bumps in the road rather than insurmountable obstacles. A well-structured plan that includes risk management techniques can help investors stay grounded even when faced with unexpected market movements.

Finally, continuous learning and adaptation play a critical role in strengthening emotional resilience. The stock market is an ever-evolving entity, influenced by various economic indicators, technological advancements, and behavioral trends. By staying informed and committed to ongoing education, investors can enhance their understanding of market dynamics, which in turn boosts their confidence in decision-making. This proactive approach not only empowers individuals to manage risk more effectively but also instills a sense of control over their investment journey, further reinforcing their emotional strength in the face of market challenges.

Techniques for Maintaining Focus During Market Turbulence

Maintaining focus during market turbulence is critical for investors seeking to navigate uncertainty without succumbing to emotional decision-making. One effective technique is to establish a well-defined investment plan that outlines specific goals and risk tolerance levels. By having a clear framework, investors can remind themselves of their long-term objectives during volatile periods, preventing impulsive reactions to short-term market fluctuations. This plan should include guidelines for asset allocation, diversification strategies, and criteria for rebalancing, which serve as anchors in tumultuous times.

Another technique is to leverage technology and analytical tools to monitor market conditions and economic indicators. By utilizing real-time data and analytics, investors can gain a clearer picture of market trends and avoid being swayed by sensationalist news or emotional biases. Tools such as risk assessment models and financial dashboards can provide insights into portfolio performance and market movements, thereby helping investors make informed decisions based on data rather than fear or speculation.

Practicing mindfulness and emotional resilience is also essential for maintaining focus. Techniques such as meditation, deep breathing exercises, or even regular physical activity can help investors manage stress and maintain a level-headed approach when market volatility peaks. By cultivating emotional awareness, investors can recognize when fear or anxiety is influencing their decisions, allowing them to step back and reassess their strategies without succumbing to panic.

Establishing a support network is another important technique. Engaging with fellow investors, financial advisors, or investment clubs can provide valuable perspectives and reinforce commitment to a disciplined investment strategy. Sharing experiences and strategies with others can create a sense of community and accountability, which can bolster confidence during uncertain times. This camaraderie can also serve as a sounding board for ideas and concerns, helping individuals stay focused on their long-term objectives.

Lastly, it is crucial to regularly review and adjust investment strategies in response to changing market conditions while staying true to the original plan. This involves not just a quarterly or annual review but also a continual assessment of economic indicators and personal financial situations. By being proactive rather than reactive, investors can better navigate periods of volatility, ensuring that they are both resilient and adaptable in the face of market turbulence. This disciplined approach fosters a mindset of preparedness, enabling investors to take rational actions rather than emotional ones as they manage their market risks.

Chapter 9: Market Risk Management for Retirement Planning

Assessing Retirement Investment Risks

Assessing retirement investment risks is a critical component of effective financial planning, especially as individuals approach the later stages of their careers. The landscape of retirement investing is fraught with uncertainties, including market volatility, inflation, and changes in personal circumstances. Understanding these risks is essential for developing a robust investment strategy that can withstand potential financial downturns while ensuring sufficient growth to meet retirement needs.

One of the primary risks to consider is market risk, which encompasses the potential for losses due to fluctuations in stock prices. As markets can be unpredictable, it is crucial for investors to assess their exposure to this risk through diversification. A well-diversified portfolio that includes various asset classes—such as stocks, bonds, and real estate—can help mitigate the impact of adverse market movements. Additionally, understanding the correlation between different investments can aid in selecting assets that may perform differently under varying market conditions.

Inflation is another significant risk that retirement investors must navigate. As the cost of living increases, the purchasing power of fixed income sources, such as pensions and social security, may decline. This necessitates a focus on growth-oriented investments that can outpace inflation over time. Investors should analyze historical inflation rates and consider incorporating inflation-protected securities or equities with strong earnings growth potential into their portfolios. This proactive approach can help secure the financial stability needed during retirement.

Behavioral finance also plays a crucial role in assessing investment risks. Investors often exhibit irrational behaviors, such as panic selling during market downturns or overconfidence in rising markets. By recognizing these behavioral tendencies, individuals can develop emotional resilience and stick to their long-term investment plans. Implementing systematic investment strategies, such as dollar-cost averaging, can help reduce the impact of emotional decision-making and encourage disciplined investing habits.

Lastly, the role of technology in assessing and managing investment risks cannot be overlooked. Various risk assessment tools and software can provide valuable insights into market trends and individual investment performance. Utilizing these technological advancements allows investors to stay informed and make data-driven decisions. Additionally, incorporating options and futures can serve as effective hedging strategies against market volatility, further enhancing the risk management framework essential for retirement planning. By comprehensively assessing and addressing these risks, individuals can better position themselves for a secure and fulfilling retirement.

Strategies for Safe Withdrawal Rates

A safe withdrawal rate is crucial for individuals looking to secure their financial future in retirement while managing market risks. The concept revolves around determining the percentage of one's retirement portfolio that can be withdrawn annually without depleting the funds over a specified period. A commonly referenced rule is the 4% rule, which suggests that retirees can withdraw 4% of their initial retirement assets each year, adjusted for inflation. However, the variability of market conditions and individual circumstances necessitates a more nuanced approach to withdrawal strategies.

One effective strategy for establishing a safe withdrawal rate is to utilize historical data to simulate various market conditions. This involves analyzing past market performance, particularly during downturns, to assess how different withdrawal rates would have fared. Investors can use Monte Carlo simulations to project the likelihood of portfolio survival over different time frames and withdrawal rates. By assessing these simulations, individuals can identify a conservative withdrawal rate that accounts for potential market volatility, thereby enhancing the sustainability of their retirement income.

Another important consideration is the diversification of assets within the retirement portfolio. A well-diversified investment strategy spreads risk across various asset classes, reducing the likelihood of significant losses that could impact withdrawal sustainability. Incorporating a mix of equities, bonds, and alternative investments allows retirees to balance growth potential with risk management. Adjusting the asset allocation based on market conditions and personal risk tolerance can further enhance the effectiveness of the withdrawal rate strategy.

Behavioral finance also plays a crucial role in determining safe withdrawal rates. Investors must remain aware of their emotional responses to market fluctuations, which can lead to impulsive decisions that jeopardize their long-term financial goals. Developing emotional resilience can help investors adhere to their withdrawal strategy, even during market downturns. Establishing a systematic withdrawal plan, rather than reacting to short-term market movements, promotes adherence to a predetermined strategy, thus enhancing financial stability.

Lastly, regular reassessment of the withdrawal strategy is vital to adapting to changing personal circumstances and market conditions. Factors such as changes in health care costs, lifestyle adjustments, and unforeseen expenses can all influence the sustainability of withdrawals. Annual reviews of the portfolio, considering both market performance and personal needs, allow retirees to make informed adjustments to their withdrawal rates. By maintaining flexibility and responsiveness to both market trends and personal circumstances, individuals can develop a robust plan that supports their financial security throughout retirement.

Adjusting Portfolios for Different Retirement Stages

Adjusting portfolios for different retirement stages is a crucial strategy for mitigating market risk and ensuring financial stability throughout one's retirement years. As individuals transition through various phases of retirement planning, their financial goals, risk tolerance, and income needs evolve. Understanding these changes and making appropriate adjustments to investment portfolios can help retirees maintain their desired lifestyle while minimizing exposure to market fluctuations.

In the early stages of retirement, individuals often have a longer time horizon for their investments, which allows for a more aggressive approach. This phase, often referred to as the "go-go years," is characterized by increased spending on travel, leisure activities, and other lifestyle enhancements. During this period, it is advisable to maintain a higher allocation to equities, as they generally offer greater potential for growth. Investors should consider diversifying their equity holdings across sectors and geographies to mitigate specific risks associated with economic downturns.

As retirees enter the "slow-go years," typically around the mid-retirement phase, their spending patterns may shift toward more conservative needs, such as healthcare and maintaining their homes. At this stage, it becomes essential to rebalance the portfolio to reduce equity exposure and increase allocations to fixed-income securities. Bonds and other income-generating assets can provide a stable cash flow that aligns with the increasing need for liquidity and capital preservation. Additionally, incorporating low-volatility stocks or income-producing investments can help manage risk while still seeking growth potential.

In the later stages of retirement, often referred to as the "no-go years," individuals generally have lower risk tolerance and a greater focus on preserving capital. During this phase, it is critical to ensure that the portfolio is not overly exposed to market volatility. A conservative asset allocation, with a significant emphasis on bonds, cash equivalents, and other safe-haven investments, becomes essential. This approach can help protect against potential market downturns and ensure that retirees have sufficient resources to cover their living expenses without the stress of fluctuating stock prices.

Ultimately, adjusting portfolios according to the various stages of retirement is not a one-time event but an ongoing process. Regular reviews and rebalancing are essential to align investments with changing financial goals and market conditions. By employing risk assessment tools and understanding individual risk tolerance, retirees can make informed decisions that safeguard their financial future. Emphasizing emotional resilience during these adjustments can further enhance the ability to navigate market uncertainties, ensuring that retirees remain focused on their long-term objectives rather than short-term market fluctuations.

Chapter 10: The Role of Technology in Predicting Market Trends

Overview of Market Analysis Tools

Market analysis tools are essential for investors looking to navigate the complex landscape of stock trading. These tools encompass a variety of methodologies and technologies designed to help individuals make informed decisions based on market data, trends, and economic indicators. By leveraging these tools, investors can assess potential risks and rewards, tailor their investment strategies, and ultimately enhance their ability to avoid significant losses in volatile markets. Understanding the different types of market analysis tools available is crucial for anyone aiming to master market risk.

One common category of market analysis tools is technical analysis software. These programs analyze historical price movements and trading volumes to identify patterns and trends that can predict future price behavior. Technical indicators, such as moving averages, Bollinger Bands, and relative strength indices, are often integrated into these tools, providing users with visual representations of market conditions. By understanding and interpreting these indicators, investors can make more precise entry and exit decisions, reducing the likelihood of emotional trading and impulsive reactions to market fluctuations.

Fundamental analysis tools represent another vital segment of market analysis. These tools focus on assessing a company's financial health, economic environment, and overall market conditions to determine its intrinsic value. Key metrics such as earnings per share, price-to-earnings ratios, and debt-to-equity ratios are commonly analyzed. Investors using fundamental analysis tools can better understand the underlying factors that drive stock prices, enabling them to make long-term investment decisions based on solid economic principles rather than short-term market sentiment.

In recent years, the role of technology in market analysis has expanded significantly. Advanced algorithms and data analytics platforms are now being utilized to process vast amounts of market data in real time. Machine learning and artificial intelligence enhance predictive capabilities, allowing for more accurate forecasting of market trends. These technological advancements not only streamline the analysis process but also empower individual investors with tools that were once only available to institutional investors. As a result, understanding and utilizing these technological tools can provide a competitive edge in risk management strategies.

Finally, emotional resilience plays a crucial role in the effective use of market analysis tools. Investors must be equipped not only with analytical skills but also with the psychological fortitude to withstand market volatility and the uncertainties inherent in investing. Tools that incorporate behavioral finance principles can assist in fostering a mindset conducive to rational decision-making. By combining robust market analysis tools with emotional resilience strategies, investors can create a comprehensive approach to managing market risk, ultimately leading to more informed and less emotionally driven investment choices.

The Rise of Artificial Intelligence in Investing

The integration of artificial intelligence (AI) into investing has transformed the landscape of financial markets, ushering in a new era of data-driven decision-making. AI technologies analyze vast amounts of market data at unprecedented speeds, allowing investors to uncover patterns and insights that were previously inaccessible. This capability extends beyond traditional analysis, enabling the identification of emerging trends and the optimization of investment strategies. As a result, investors are increasingly relying on AI tools to enhance their understanding of market dynamics and to mitigate risks associated with stock market fluctuations.

One of the key advantages of AI in investing is its ability to process and analyze unstructured data. Traditional financial analysis often focuses on quantitative data, such as earnings reports and stock prices; however, AI can also incorporate qualitative factors, including news articles, social media sentiment, and macroeconomic indicators. By synthesizing this diverse range of information, AI-driven algorithms can provide a more comprehensive view of market sentiment and potential future movements. This multifaceted approach aids investors in making informed decisions that align with their risk tolerance and investment goals.

Moreover, the rise of machine learning has further enhanced the capabilities of AI in finance. Machine learning algorithms learn from historical data, identifying correlations and patterns that may not be immediately apparent to human analysts. These algorithms can adapt to changing market conditions, enabling them to refine their predictive models continuously. As they evolve, these AI tools can better anticipate market shifts, allowing investors to adjust their strategies proactively. This adaptability is crucial in an environment where market volatility can lead to substantial losses if not managed effectively.

AI also plays a significant role in risk assessment and portfolio diversification. By simulating various market scenarios and stress-testing investment portfolios, AI tools can help investors understand potential vulnerabilities and optimize their asset allocations. This capability is particularly valuable for individual investors who may lack the resources to conduct extensive risk analyses. With AI, they can access sophisticated risk management strategies that enhance the resilience of their portfolios against market downturns.

As the use of AI in investing continues to grow, it is essential for investors to remain informed about the technology's limitations and ethical implications. While AI can significantly enhance decision-making processes, it is crucial to maintain a balance between human judgment and machine assistance. Investors should also be aware of potential biases in AI algorithms that could skew results. By understanding both the strengths and weaknesses of AI, investors can leverage these tools effectively while maintaining a robust risk management framework that safeguards their financial futures.

Leveraging Data Analytics for Better Decision-Making

In today's data-driven investment landscape, leveraging data analytics has become essential for making informed decisions in stock market trading. Investors can utilize data analytics to interpret vast amounts of information, identify trends, and forecast potential market movements. By transforming raw data into actionable insights, investors can reduce uncertainty and enhance their decision-making processes. This is particularly relevant for individual investors who may lack the resources of larger institutional players but can still harness sophisticated analytical tools to level the playing field.

One of the key advantages of data analytics is its ability to provide a comprehensive view of market conditions. By analyzing historical price movements, trading volumes, and economic indicators, investors can discern patterns that may not be immediately visible. For instance, correlation analysis can reveal relationships between different stocks or sectors, allowing investors to make more strategic choices in diversifying their portfolios. Furthermore, understanding these correlations helps in assessing the potential impact of macroeconomic changes on individual investments, thereby informing risk management strategies.

Behavioral finance plays a significant role in understanding how psychological factors influence investment decisions. Data analytics can help mitigate biases by providing objective data that challenges emotional decision-making. For example, sentiment analysis can gauge market sentiment from news articles, social media, and other digital platforms, offering insights into how public perception may affect stock prices. By integrating this data into their decision-making processes, investors can combat herd mentality and make choices grounded in factual analysis rather than emotional impulses.

Additionally, the use of predictive analytics can significantly enhance an investor's ability to anticipate market shifts. Machine learning algorithms can analyze historical data to identify potential future trends, offering insights that can inform both short-term trading strategies and long-term investment planning. Tools that forecast economic indicators, such as unemployment rates or inflation, can further equip investors to adjust their portfolios proactively in response to anticipated market changes. This forward-looking approach is crucial for managing risk and optimizing investment returns.

Ultimately, the integration of data analytics into investment strategies empowers investors to navigate the complexities of the stock market more effectively. By embracing technology and analytical tools, investors can better understand their risk tolerance and align their strategies with their financial goals. As the market continues to evolve, those who master the art of utilizing data analytics will be better positioned to minimize losses, capitalize on opportunities, and achieve long-term success in their investment endeavors.

Chapter 11: Case Studies of Successful Risk Management in Investing

Learning from Market Leaders

Learning from market leaders provides invaluable insights into effective strategies for managing risks associated with stock market investing. Market leaders, often characterized by their ability to navigate volatile environments, serve as models for both individual and institutional investors. By examining their approaches, investors can glean lessons on risk assessment, portfolio diversification, and the importance of emotional resilience. These leaders not only demonstrate the significance of strategic planning but also highlight the necessity of adapting to changing market conditions.

One key takeaway from successful market leaders is the implementation of rigorous risk assessment tools. They prioritize thorough analysis and data-driven decision-making, allowing them to identify potential pitfalls before they become critical issues. These tools, which range from quantitative models to qualitative assessments, empower investors to evaluate their portfolios effectively. By incorporating such methodologies, individual investors can reduce exposure to market volatility and make informed decisions that align with their financial goals.

Another aspect that market leaders excel in is diversification. They understand that spreading investments across various asset classes can mitigate risk significantly. By diversifying their portfolios, they can cushion against downturns in specific sectors or securities. This lesson is particularly relevant for individual investors, who may be tempted to concentrate their investments in a few high-performing stocks. Learning from market leaders encourages a more balanced approach that encompasses a wider array of investments, thereby enhancing overall portfolio stability.

Emotional resilience is another critical factor that market leaders exhibit in their investment strategies. They maintain discipline and composure, especially during periods of market turmoil. This emotional strength allows them to stick to their strategies, avoiding impulsive decisions driven by fear or greed. Individual investors can benefit from cultivating similar resilience, as emotional reactions can often lead to detrimental choices, particularly in volatile markets. Developing a personal risk tolerance framework that accounts for psychological factors can help investors remain steadfast in their strategies.

Finally, the role of technology in predicting market trends cannot be overlooked. Market leaders leverage advanced analytics and algorithms to anticipate shifts in market dynamics. This technological advantage aids in making well-informed investment decisions and adjusting strategies proactively. Individual investors should embrace these technological tools to enhance their market understanding and improve their risk management practices. By integrating technology with traditional investment philosophies, they can better position themselves in a competitive and ever-changing market landscape.

Analyzing Failures and Successes

Analyzing failures and successes in the stock market is crucial for investors aiming to master market risk. Each investment decision carries inherent uncertainties, and understanding the reasons behind both failures and successes can provide valuable insights for future strategies. By dissecting past experiences—whether personal or observed in broader market trends—investors can identify patterns that inform their approaches to risk management. This analysis not only enhances decision-making but also helps in developing a personal risk tolerance framework that aligns with individual investment goals.

Failures often serve as the most instructive learning opportunities. Historical case studies illustrate that many successful investors have

faced significant setbacks before achieving their goals. For example, examining the dot-com bubble reveals that many investors were lured by hype without adequate risk assessment, leading to devastating losses. By analyzing such failures, investors can recognize the importance of thorough research, understanding economic indicators, and maintaining a diversified portfolio to mitigate risks. This awareness can foster a more cautious and strategic mindset, enabling individuals to avoid similar pitfalls in their investment journeys.

Conversely, the analysis of successful investment strategies provides a roadmap for achieving favorable outcomes. Investors who have effectively navigated market fluctuations often share common practices such as disciplined risk assessment, emotional resilience, and the use of hedging techniques like options and futures. These elements of successful investing can be dissected to reveal actionable strategies that others can adopt. For instance, a detailed study of portfolios that thrived during economic downturns can highlight the benefits of diversification and the strategic allocation of resources across various asset classes.

Behavioral finance plays a pivotal role in understanding both failures and successes in the stock market. Psychological factors often influence investment decisions, leading to irrational behaviors that can exacerbate losses or hinder gains. Analyzing these behaviors provides insight into the emotional resilience necessary for trading, allowing investors to develop strategies to counteract cognitive biases. By fostering a deep awareness of one's own emotional responses to market movements, investors can cultivate a more rational approach to decision-making, ultimately enhancing their ability to navigate market risks.

In conclusion, the continuous process of analyzing failures and successes is essential for investors who aspire to master market risk. By learning from past mistakes and successes, individuals can refine their investment strategies, bolster their understanding of market dynamics, and enhance their overall risk management capabilities. This ongoing evaluation not only contributes to personal growth as an investor but also prepares individuals for the complexities and unpredictabilities of the stock market. Ultimately, a reflective approach to investment can lead to more informed decisions that align with one's financial aspirations and risk tolerance.

Key Takeaways from Real-World Examples

Real-world examples of market risk management provide invaluable insights into effective strategies and potential pitfalls that investors may encounter. By analyzing these case studies, individuals can draw key takeaways that enhance their understanding of market dynamics and inform their investment decisions. One notable example is the 2008 financial crisis, which underscored the importance of robust risk assessment tools. Investors who relied on comprehensive analyses of market indicators and financial health were better positioned to mitigate losses during the downturn. This highlights the necessity for individual investors to adopt a disciplined approach to evaluating economic indicators, ensuring they remain aware of the broader market context.

Another critical lesson emerges from the behavior of investors during volatile market periods. Many experienced significant emotional distress, leading to hasty decisions that exacerbated their losses. Behavioral finance studies illustrate that emotional resilience plays a key role in successful investing. Investors who maintained a long-term perspective and adhered to their strategic plans typically fared better than those who reacted impulsively to market fluctuations. This emphasizes the need for developing a personal risk tolerance framework, allowing investors to navigate uncertainty with greater confidence and composure.

Diversification remains one of the most effective strategies for managing market risk, as evidenced by numerous successful investment portfolios. Case studies reveal that investors who spread their assets across various sectors and asset classes were less vulnerable to downturns in any single market segment. This reinforces the importance of not only diversifying stock portfolios but also considering alternative investments such as options and futures. These tools can offer additional layers of protection, allowing investors to hedge against potential losses in their core holdings.

The role of technology in predicting market trends has also been highlighted through real-world examples. Advanced analytics and algorithmic trading have transformed the investment landscape, enabling investors to access real-time data and make informed decisions. Successful investors leverage these technological tools to enhance their market predictions and risk assessments. However, it is essential to complement technology with sound judgment and an understanding of market fundamentals, as reliance solely on algorithms may overlook critical qualitative factors influencing market movements.

In summary, examining real-world examples provides essential takeaways for mastering market risk. The importance of rigorous risk assessment, emotional resilience, diversification, and the effective use of technology cannot be overstated. By learning from the experiences of others, investors can develop strategies that not only protect their investments but also position them for long-term success in the stock market. Emphasizing these principles will foster a more informed and resilient approach to navigating the complexities of market risk.

Chapter 12: Developing a Personal Risk Tolerance Framework

Defining Your Investment Goals and Timeline

Defining investment goals and timelines is critical for successful investing, particularly in a landscape rife with market risk. Clear goals act as a roadmap for your investment journey, guiding decisions and strategies. Whether you are saving for retirement, planning a significant purchase, or simply aiming to grow your wealth, understanding what you want to achieve is the first step. Each goal will have a different timeline and risk tolerance associated with it, influencing the types of investments you choose and the strategies you employ.

When setting your investment goals, it is essential to be specific and realistic. Goals should be measurable and time-bound, allowing you to track your progress effectively. For instance, rather than stating a general desire to "make money," articulate that you wish to accumulate a certain amount within a defined period, such as saving $100,000 for retirement in 20 years. This specificity not only clarifies your objectives but also helps in evaluating the necessary steps and investment strategies required to reach those goals.

The timeline associated with your investment goals plays a significant role in shaping your overall investment strategy. Short-term goals, typically defined as those expected to be achieved within five years, often require a more conservative approach to minimize risk. Conversely, long-term goals, like retirement savings, can afford to take on more risk, as there is more time to recover from market downturns. Investors must align their asset allocation with their timeline to optimize returns while managing risk effectively.

Behavioral finance also plays a crucial role in how investors define their goals and timelines. Investors often fall prey to cognitive biases that can distort their perception of risk and reward. Recognizing these biases is essential for setting realistic and achievable goals. For example, the optimism bias might lead an investor to underestimate potential market downturns, while loss aversion might cause them to avoid necessary risk-taking. By acknowledging these psychological factors, investors can better align their goals with a realistic assessment of market conditions.

Ultimately, defining your investment goals and timeline is an ongoing process. As you navigate the complexities of the market, it is vital to regularly reassess your objectives and the strategies employed to achieve them. Changes in personal circumstances, financial markets, or economic indicators may necessitate adjustments to your plan. By maintaining flexibility and being open to reevaluating your goals, you can better position yourself to manage market risk and avoid stock market losses.

Assessing Personal Risk Appetite

Assessing personal risk appetite is a crucial step for any investor looking to navigate the complexities of the stock market effectively. Personal risk appetite refers to the level of risk an individual is willing to accept when investing, which can vary significantly from person to person. Understanding one's risk appetite is essential for making informed investment decisions, as it influences asset allocation, investment strategy, and overall portfolio management. Investors must recognize that their risk appetite is shaped not only by financial circumstances but also by psychological factors, life experiences, and individual investment goals.

To begin assessing personal risk appetite, investors should conduct a thorough self-assessment. This involves evaluating their financial situation, including income, savings, current investments, and long-term financial goals. Additionally, considering factors such as age, investment horizon, and obligations can provide valuable insight into how much risk is appropriate. For instance, younger investors may have a higher risk tolerance due to a longer time frame for recovery from potential losses, whereas those nearing retirement may prefer more conservative investments to protect their capital.

Another essential aspect of assessing risk appetite is understanding emotional responses to market fluctuations. Behavioral finance plays a significant role in how investors react to gains and losses. Some individuals may be more prone to panic during market downturns, leading to hasty decisions that can exacerbate losses. By recognizing their emotional triggers and biases, investors can better align their investment strategies with their true risk tolerance. Tools such as risk assessment questionnaires can help quantify emotional responses and provide a clearer picture of personal risk appetite.

Creating a personal risk tolerance framework is also vital for effective risk management. This framework should encompass both qualitative and quantitative measures of risk, allowing investors to establish clear guidelines for their investment decisions. Factors to consider include the types of assets in the portfolio, the volatility of those assets, and the investor's capacity to withstand potential losses. Regularly revisiting and adjusting this framework as financial situations and market conditions change ensures that it remains relevant and effective.

Finally, the role of technology cannot be overlooked in assessing personal risk appetite. Various digital tools and platforms offer sophisticated risk assessment capabilities, providing personalized insights based on historical data and market trends. Investors can leverage these technologies to simulate different market scenarios and understand potential risks associated with their investment choices. By integrating technology into their risk assessment processes, investors can enhance their decision-making, ultimately leading to more resilient and diversified portfolios that are better equipped to withstand market fluctuations.

Creating a Dynamic Risk Tolerance Plan

Creating a dynamic risk tolerance plan is essential for investors seeking to navigate the uncertainties of the stock market effectively. A well-structured risk tolerance plan not only helps in identifying an investor's comfort level with potential losses but also guides decision-making throughout various market conditions. The first step in building this plan involves a thorough self-assessment of financial goals, investment horizon, and personal circumstances. Investors must ask themselves what they aim to achieve with their investments and how much risk they are willing to endure to reach those objectives.

Once investors have a clear understanding of their goals, the next step involves analyzing their financial situation, which includes assessing income, expenses, assets, and liabilities. This comprehensive assessment will enable investors to determine their capacity for risk. A key component of this analysis is understanding the impact of market fluctuations on their overall financial health. By evaluating how different levels of market risk could affect their financial stability, investors can better align their investment strategies with their risk tolerance.

Incorporating behavioral finance principles into the risk tolerance plan is crucial for addressing emotional responses to market movements. Investors often react to market volatility with fear or greed, which can lead to impulsive decisions that contradict their long-term strategies. Creating a dynamic risk tolerance plan requires an awareness of these behavioral tendencies and strategies to mitigate their effects. Techniques such as setting predefined loss limits and establishing a systematic approach to portfolio rebalancing can help maintain discipline during turbulent market periods.

Diversification is another vital element of a dynamic risk tolerance plan. By spreading investments across various asset classes, sectors, and geographies, investors can reduce the impact of volatility on their overall portfolio. A diversified approach allows for a more stable return profile, which can align better with an investor's risk tolerance. Regularly reviewing and adjusting the diversification strategy in response to changing market conditions and personal circumstances can further enhance risk management efforts.

Finally, technology plays a significant role in developing and implementing a dynamic risk tolerance plan. Utilizing risk assessment tools and analytic software can provide valuable insights into market trends and individual portfolio performance. These tools can aid in scenario analysis, helping investors understand potential outcomes based on different risk levels. By integrating technology into their risk management processes, investors can make more informed decisions and adapt their strategies to evolving market dynamics, ensuring that their risk tolerance plan remains robust and effective over time.

Navigating Market Turbulence: Strategies to Protect Your Investments

Chapter 1: Understanding Market Turbulence

The Nature of Market Fluctuations

Market fluctuations are a fundamental characteristic of economic systems, driven by a myriad of factors including investor sentiment, economic indicators, and geopolitical events. At their core, these fluctuations arise from the basic principles of supply and demand. When more investors want to buy stocks than sell them, prices rise. Conversely, when more investors wish to sell than buy, prices fall. Understanding this dynamic is crucial for investors looking to navigate the complexities of the market and mitigate risks associated with sudden price changes.

One of the key elements contributing to market fluctuations is investor psychology. The collective mood of investors often dictates market movements, leading to phenomena such as bull and bear markets. During bullish phases, optimism prevails, and prices tend to increase as investors anticipate higher future earnings. However, bear markets are characterized by pessimism, where fear and uncertainty can lead to rapid sell-offs. This psychological aspect can sometimes create price movements that are disconnected from fundamental valuations, making it imperative for investors to maintain a level-headed approach during periods of volatility.

Economic indicators also play a significant role in influencing market fluctuations. Data such as unemployment rates, inflation figures, and GDP growth can signal the health of the economy and, in turn, affect investor confidence. For instance, a sudden rise in inflation may prompt fears of interest rate hikes by central banks, leading to a sell-off in stocks as investors reposition their portfolios. Conversely, positive economic news can boost market sentiment and drive stock prices higher. Staying informed about these indicators is essential for investors aiming to anticipate and respond to potential market shifts effectively.

Geopolitical events can introduce additional layers of complexity to market fluctuations. Events such as elections, international conflicts, or trade negotiations can create uncertainty, prompting investors to react swiftly to news and developments. For example, tensions in a major oil-producing region may lead to fluctuations in energy stocks, while changes in trade policy can impact companies reliant on international supply chains. Understanding the broader geopolitical landscape is vital for investors, as these events can lead to sudden and significant market movements that might not correlate with traditional economic indicators.

In conclusion, market fluctuations are an inherent aspect of investing, influenced by investor psychology, economic indicators, and geopolitical events. For those mastering market risk, recognizing the nature of these fluctuations is essential for developing strategies to protect investments. By remaining informed and adaptable, investors can better navigate the turbulence of market cycles, positioning themselves to safeguard their portfolios against unforeseen changes. Embracing a disciplined approach, informed by both data and market sentiment, will ultimately enhance the resilience of investment strategies in the face of inevitable fluctuation.

Historical Context of Market Crises

The historical context of market crises provides valuable insights for investors looking to protect their portfolios. Market crises are often triggered by a combination of economic, political, and social factors that create an environment of instability. Analyzing past crises reveals patterns that can help investors anticipate potential risks and adapt their strategies accordingly. Understanding these events is crucial for mastering market risk and avoiding significant losses in turbulent times.

One of the most notable market crises occurred during the Great Depression of the 1930s. This period was marked by widespread bank failures, massive unemployment, and a plummeting stock market. The stock market crash of 1929, which preceded the Great Depression, was fueled by speculative investments and an overheated economy. As panic set in, investors rushed to sell their stocks, leading to a sharp decline in prices. This historical event serves as a reminder of the dangers of speculation and the importance of maintaining a diversified portfolio to mitigate risk.

The 2008 financial crisis offers another critical case study for understanding market crises. Triggered by the collapse of the housing bubble and the subsequent failure of major financial institutions, this crisis highlighted the interconnectedness of global markets and the impact of poor regulatory oversight. The resulting recession led to significant declines in stock prices and widespread economic hardship. Analyzing the causes and consequences of this crisis underscores the necessity for investors to remain vigilant about market conditions and the broader economic landscape.

In addition to these significant historical events, smaller market disruptions have also shaped the investment landscape. Factors such as geopolitical tensions, natural disasters, and technological advancements can lead to abrupt market shifts. For instance, the dot-com bubble in the late 1990s was driven by speculative investments in technology companies, which ultimately led to a market correction. Investors who failed to recognize the signs of an overheated market faced substantial losses. Learning from these instances emphasizes the importance of continuous market analysis and risk assessment.

Ultimately, understanding the historical context of market crises equips investors with the knowledge to navigate future turbulence. By studying past events, investors can identify potential warning signs and implement proactive strategies to safeguard their investments. This historical perspective not only enhances risk management but also fosters a more resilient investment approach, enabling individuals to weather market fluctuations with greater confidence.

Key Indicators of Market Turbulence

Market turbulence can be identified through several key indicators that serve as warning signs for investors. Understanding these indicators is essential for anyone looking to navigate the complex landscape of financial markets. One of the primary indicators is volatility, often measured by the VIX index, which reflects the market's expectations of future volatility based on options pricing. A rising VIX typically signals increased uncertainty and potential market declines, alerting investors to reassess their positions. Monitoring fluctuations in the VIX can provide early warnings of turbulent conditions, allowing for timely adjustments in investment strategies.

Another critical indicator is trading volume, which can reveal shifts in market sentiment. During periods of turbulence, trading volumes may spike as investors react to news or economic data. High volume can indicate strong conviction in market direction, whether bullish or bearish. Conversely, low trading volume during price declines may suggest a lack of confidence among investors, signaling that the downward trend could continue. By analyzing trading volume alongside price movements, investors can gain insights into the strength and sustainability of market trends.

Economic indicators play a significant role in assessing market turbulence as well. Key metrics such as GDP growth rates, unemployment figures, and inflation indices can influence investor sentiment and market stability. For instance, if economic data reveals a slowdown in growth or rising unemployment, it may trigger a market sell-off as investors foresee potential downturns. Keeping abreast of economic reports and central bank announcements can help investors anticipate market shifts and adjust their strategies accordingly.

Geopolitical events are another vital factor that can lead to market turbulence. Political instability, trade disputes, and international conflicts can create uncertainty in the markets, prompting investors to reassess risk exposure. Events such as elections, policy changes, or sanctions can have immediate and far-reaching implications for market performance. Investors should stay informed about global events and their potential impact on market dynamics to make informed decisions during turbulent times.

Lastly, sentiment indicators, such as consumer confidence surveys and investor sentiment indices, can provide valuable insights into market psychology. High levels of optimism may precede market corrections, while extreme pessimism can indicate potential buying opportunities. By tracking sentiment indicators, investors can gauge the prevailing mood in the market and identify potential turning points. Understanding these key indicators of market turbulence allows investors to navigate risks more effectively and protect their investments during uncertain times.

Chapter 2: Risk Assessment and Management

Identifying Your Risk Tolerance

Understanding your risk tolerance is a fundamental aspect of navigating market turbulence effectively. Risk tolerance refers to the degree of variability in investment returns that an individual is willing to withstand. It is influenced by various factors, including financial situation, investment goals, and emotional capacity to handle market fluctuations. Identifying your risk tolerance is crucial because it helps tailor your investment strategy to align with your comfort level and financial objectives, ultimately guiding you toward more informed decision-making.

One of the primary factors to consider when assessing risk tolerance is your financial situation. This includes your income, savings, debts, and overall financial stability. Individuals with a secure financial base and substantial savings may be more able to withstand short-term volatility compared to someone with limited financial resources. A thorough analysis of your current financial standing will provide insights into how much risk you can afford to take without jeopardizing your financial security. It is essential to create a comprehensive view of your finances, taking into account not just your assets but also your obligations.

Investment goals also play a significant role in determining risk tolerance. Different financial objectives require different strategies and levels of risk. For example, if you are saving for retirement that is several decades away, you might adopt a more aggressive investment approach, as you have time to recover from potential losses. Conversely, if your goal is to fund a child's education in the next few years, a more conservative strategy may be warranted to preserve capital. Clearly defining your investment goals will help in aligning your risk tolerance with your desired outcomes.

Emotional capacity is another critical component in the risk tolerance equation. Market fluctuations can evoke strong emotional responses, and recognizing how you typically react to financial stress can inform your investment decisions. Some investors may panic during downturns, leading to rash decisions such as selling off assets at a loss. Others may remain calm and stick to their long-term strategies despite market volatility. Self-reflection and honesty about your emotional resilience in the face of market challenges can help determine an appropriate risk level for your portfolio.

Finally, it is advisable to conduct regular assessments of your risk tolerance as personal circumstances and market conditions change. Life events such as marriage, having children, or nearing retirement can all impact your financial situation and emotional readiness for risk. Additionally, shifts in the market environment may require an adjustment in your investment approach. By periodically reviewing your risk tolerance, you can ensure that your investment strategy remains aligned with both your financial goals and personal comfort levels, ultimately enhancing your ability to navigate market turbulence successfully.

Tools for Risk Assessment

Risk assessment is a critical component of investment strategy, particularly in turbulent market conditions. Investors must be equipped with the right tools to identify, analyze, and mitigate risks effectively. A variety of methodologies and technologies are available that can enhance the risk assessment process. These tools range from qualitative assessments to quantitative models, each offering unique insights into potential vulnerabilities within an investment portfolio. Understanding these tools is essential for mastering market risk and protecting investments from unforeseen downturns.

One of the fundamental tools for risk assessment is the use of financial ratios and metrics. Ratios such as the Sharpe ratio, beta, and standard deviation provide investors with a quantitative measure of an investment's risk relative to its expected return. The Sharpe ratio, for instance, evaluates the performance of an investment by adjusting for its risk, allowing investors to compare different assets on a risk-adjusted basis. Similarly, beta measures an asset's volatility in relation to the market, offering insights into how much risk an investor is taking compared to broad market movements. By utilizing these metrics, investors can make more informed decisions that align with their risk tolerance and investment objectives.

Another essential tool in the risk assessment arsenal is scenario analysis. This method involves assessing the impact of various hypothetical events on an investment portfolio. By creating different scenarios, such as economic downturns, interest rate changes, or geopolitical events, investors can evaluate potential outcomes and their implications for portfolio performance. Scenario analysis encourages proactive thinking and allows investors to develop contingency plans in advance. This foresight is crucial in navigating market turbulence, as it equips investors with the knowledge to respond quickly to adverse conditions.

Stress testing is a complementary tool that helps investors understand how their portfolios might perform under extreme conditions. Unlike scenario analysis, which often considers a range of plausible outcomes, stress testing focuses on severe market events. By applying historical data from past crises or simulated extreme market conditions, investors can gauge the potential impact of significant shocks on their investments. This process helps identify weaknesses in a portfolio and facilitates adjustments that can mitigate risks. Stress testing is particularly valuable in uncertain markets, where the likelihood of abrupt changes is heightened.

Finally, technology plays an increasingly important role in risk assessment. Advanced analytics, machine learning, and artificial intelligence can process vast amounts of data to identify patterns and anomalies that may indicate potential risks. These tools can also automate the monitoring of investment portfolios, providing real-time alerts when certain thresholds are breached. By leveraging technology, investors can enhance their risk assessment capabilities, enabling them to stay ahead of market fluctuations and make timely decisions. As the investment landscape continues to evolve, the integration of these technological tools into risk assessment strategies will be vital for maintaining a competitive edge in managing market risk.

Developing a Personalized Risk Management Plan

Developing a personalized risk management plan is crucial for investors who seek to navigate the complexities of market fluctuations effectively. The first step in crafting this plan involves assessing individual risk tolerance. Risk tolerance is influenced by various factors, including financial goals, investment horizon, and psychological comfort with market volatility. Investors should take the time to evaluate their capacity to absorb potential losses while aligning their investment strategies with their overall financial objectives. This self-assessment lays the groundwork for making informed decisions that reflect personal circumstances and preferences.

Once an investor understands their risk tolerance, the next step is to identify specific risks associated with their investment portfolio. These risks may include market risk, credit risk, liquidity risk, and interest rate risk. Investors should analyze their current holdings and recognize which of these risks are most relevant to their situation. For instance, those heavily invested in equities may face heightened market risk, while investors in bonds should be aware of interest rate fluctuations. By identifying these risks, investors can develop targeted strategies to mitigate them, ensuring a more resilient portfolio.

Diversification is a fundamental component of any effective risk management plan. By spreading investments across various asset classes, sectors, and geographical regions, investors can reduce the impact of adverse market movements on their overall portfolio. A well-diversified portfolio can cushion against the volatility of individual investments, allowing for smoother performance over time. Investors should consider their unique circumstances when determining the appropriate level of diversification, ensuring that their approach aligns with their risk tolerance and long-term goals.

Incorporating risk management tools and techniques is essential for enhancing the effectiveness of a personalized plan. Investors may employ stop-loss orders, options, or hedging strategies to protect their portfolios from significant downturns. Additionally, regular portfolio reviews are vital to ensure that the risk management plan remains relevant as market conditions change. Investors should adjust their strategies in response to shifts in market dynamics or changes in their personal circumstances, such as income fluctuations or approaching retirement. This proactive approach helps maintain alignment between risk management practices and individual objectives.

Finally, education and continuous learning play a pivotal role in the development of a personalized risk management plan. Investors should stay informed about market trends, economic indicators, and emerging risks that could impact their portfolios. Attending seminars, reading relevant literature, and engaging with financial advisors can enhance their understanding of risk management concepts and best practices. By fostering a mindset of continuous improvement and adaptability, investors can refine their risk management strategies over time, positioning themselves for greater success in the face of market turbulence.

Chapter 3: Diversification Strategies

The Importance of Diversification

Diversification is a fundamental strategy in risk management that involves spreading investments across various asset classes, sectors, and geographical regions. This approach aims to reduce the overall risk in a portfolio by mitigating the impact of any single investment's poor performance. By not putting all your eggs in one basket, investors can better withstand market volatility and enhance the potential for returns. In turbulent market conditions, where uncertainties can lead to significant losses, diversification becomes even more critical.

One of the primary reasons diversification is vital is its ability to minimize the impact of market fluctuations. Different asset classes often respond differently to economic changes. For instance, while equities may suffer during a recession, bonds might perform better, providing a buffer for the overall portfolio. Additionally, certain sectors may thrive under specific economic conditions; for example, technology stocks may excel during periods of innovation, while utility stocks typically offer stability during downturns. By incorporating a mix of assets, investors can create a more resilient portfolio that is less susceptible to the whims of the market.

Moreover, diversification helps in optimizing returns. While it may seem counterintuitive, spreading investments across various assets can lead to more stable and potentially higher returns in the long run. This is because different investments often have varying risk and return profiles. By balancing high-risk, high-reward assets with more stable investments, investors can harness the growth potential of aggressive assets while safeguarding against large losses. This strategic balance is particularly important in volatile markets, where the performance of individual stocks can be unpredictable.

Investors should also consider geographical diversification as part of their overall strategy. Economic conditions, political stability, and market performance can vary significantly from one country to another. By investing in international markets, investors can take advantage of growth opportunities that may not be available domestically. Additionally, geopolitical events that adversely affect one region may not impact another, further reducing risk. This global approach to diversification allows investors to tap into emerging markets or industries that may offer significant upside potential.

Finally, it is essential to recognize that diversification is not a one-time effort but a continuous process. As market conditions change, so do the dynamics of various asset classes. Regularly reviewing and rebalancing a portfolio ensures that it remains aligned with an investor's risk tolerance and financial goals. This ongoing attention to diversification can help mitigate risks and adapt to changing market landscapes. In essence, a well-diversified portfolio is a dynamic entity that evolves in response to both market trends and individual investment objectives, offering a stronger defense against the uncertainties inherent in investing.

Different Asset Classes for Diversification

Diversification is a fundamental strategy for managing risk in investment portfolios. Different asset classes offer unique characteristics and performance traits, allowing investors to spread their risk and potentially enhance returns. By understanding the various asset classes available, investors can make informed decisions that align with their financial goals, risk tolerance, and market conditions. The primary asset classes include equities, fixed income, real estate, commodities, and cash equivalents, each contributing differently to the overall risk-reward profile of a portfolio.

Equities, or stocks, represent ownership in a company and are typically considered a higher-risk asset class due to their volatility. Over the long term, equities have historically provided higher returns compared to other asset classes, but they are also subject to market fluctuations and economic cycles. Investors can diversify their equity exposure by investing in various sectors, geographies, and company sizes, which can help mitigate risks associated with individual stocks or specific market segments.

Fixed income investments, such as bonds, provide a steadier income stream and are generally considered safer than equities. They tend to have an inverse relationship with stocks, meaning when stock prices fall, bond prices may rise, providing a cushion during market downturns. Investors can choose from government bonds, corporate bonds, and municipal bonds, each with varying levels of risk and return. Incorporating fixed income into a portfolio can help stabilize returns and reduce overall volatility.

Real estate is another asset class that offers diversification benefits. Real estate investments can take various forms, including direct ownership of properties, real estate investment trusts (REITs), and real estate crowdfunding. These investments often provide passive income and can act as a hedge against inflation. As real estate values tend to move independently of stock and bond markets, adding real estate to a portfolio can enhance diversification and reduce risk during periods of market turbulence.

Commodities, such as gold, oil, and agricultural products, can also play a critical role in diversification strategies. Commodities have a unique correlation with economic cycles and can serve as a hedge against inflation and currency fluctuations. They often perform well in times of geopolitical uncertainty or when stock markets are underperforming. By including commodities in an investment portfolio, investors can further spread risk and enhance their potential for returns in diverse market conditions.

Lastly, cash equivalents, including money market funds and short-term government securities, provide liquidity and stability. While they offer lower returns compared to other asset classes, they are essential for maintaining flexibility in a portfolio. During periods of market volatility, having cash on hand allows investors to capitalize on opportunities without having to sell other investments at a loss.

Balancing these different asset classes is crucial for effective diversification, helping investors navigate market turbulence while protecting their investments.

Geographic and Sector Diversification

Geographic and sector diversification are critical components of an investment strategy designed to mitigate risk and enhance long-term returns. By spreading investments across various geographic regions and sectors, investors can reduce their exposure to localized economic downturns and sector-specific volatility. This approach allows for capturing growth opportunities in different markets and industries, which can be particularly beneficial during periods of market turbulence.

Geographic diversification involves allocating assets across different countries and regions. This strategy helps to hedge against country-specific risks such as political instability, economic downturns, or natural disasters. For instance, if an investor is heavily concentrated in one country and that country experiences a recession, the portfolio may suffer significant losses. By diversifying geographically, the investor can offset potential losses in one region with gains in another, thereby stabilizing overall portfolio performance. Additionally, investing in emerging markets can provide access to higher growth rates, further enhancing potential returns.

Sector diversification focuses on spreading investments across various industry sectors, such as technology, healthcare, finance, and consumer goods. Different sectors often perform differently under varying economic conditions. For example, during economic expansions, cyclical sectors like consumer discretionary tend to perform well, while defensive sectors like utilities may lag. Conversely, during recessions, defensive sectors may provide more stability. By diversifying across sectors, investors can reduce the impact of poor performance in any single industry on their overall portfolio. This balance helps in maintaining more consistent returns over time.

Implementing geographic and sector diversification requires careful analysis and ongoing monitoring. Investors should assess the correlation between different regions and sectors to ensure that their diversification strategy effectively reduces risk. While diversifying, it is essential to avoid overexposure to any single region or sector, which can negate the benefits of diversification. Tools such as exchange-traded funds (ETFs) and mutual funds can facilitate this process, allowing investors to gain exposure to a broad range of assets without needing to manage each investment individually.

In conclusion, geographic and sector diversification are vital strategies for navigating market turbulence and protecting investments. By thoughtfully spreading investments across different regions and industries, investors can better manage risks and capitalize on growth opportunities. This approach not only helps to mitigate the adverse effects of market volatility but also fosters a more resilient investment portfolio capable of withstanding economic fluctuations.

Chapter 4: Defensive Investment Strategies

Value Investing in Turbulent Times

Value investing, a strategy focused on identifying undervalued stocks with solid fundamentals, can be particularly effective during turbulent market conditions. When market volatility increases, fear often drives stock prices down, creating opportunities for astute investors who are willing to look beyond the noise. This approach requires a disciplined assessment of a company's intrinsic value compared to its market price, allowing investors to capitalize on mispriced assets. In such times, patience and thorough analysis can yield significant rewards, as markets tend to correct themselves over the long term.

During periods of economic uncertainty, many investors flee to safety, causing a broad sell-off that can disproportionately affect fundamentally sound companies. Value investors can take advantage of this panic by identifying stocks that have strong balance sheets, consistent earnings, and competitive advantages, yet are trading at discounts. Performance metrics such as price-to-earnings ratios, price-to-book ratios, and dividend yields become essential tools in this analysis. By focusing on these indicators, investors can uncover hidden gems that the market has overlooked, positioning themselves for future growth once stability returns.

Moreover, the discipline of value investing emphasizes a long-term perspective, which is crucial in turbulent times. While market fluctuations can prompt knee-jerk reactions, value investors who adhere to a well-defined investment thesis are less likely to be swayed by short-term volatility. This steadfastness allows them to endure market downturns without selling off their positions at a loss. By maintaining a focus on intrinsic value, investors can weather the storm, knowing that their investments are grounded in thorough research and sound financial principles.

Additionally, diversification plays a pivotal role in value investing strategies during uncertain times. By spreading investments across various sectors and industries, value investors can mitigate risks associated with individual stock volatility. This approach not only helps in reducing potential losses but also increases the likelihood of capturing upside potential from different market segments as recovery begins. A well-diversified portfolio that includes defensive stocks, dividend-paying companies, and emerging growth sectors can provide a buffer against market shocks while still aligning with a value-oriented strategy.

Lastly, understanding the broader economic landscape is vital for successful value investing in turbulent times. Factors such as interest rates, inflationary pressures, and geopolitical events can significantly influence market dynamics. Staying informed about these elements allows investors to make more informed decisions regarding their value investments. By analyzing macroeconomic indicators and adjusting their strategies accordingly, value investors can enhance their ability to navigate market turbulence, ensuring that they not only protect their investments but also position themselves to benefit from the eventual market recovery.

The Role of Bonds and Fixed Income

Bonds and fixed income investments play a crucial role in a well-rounded investment strategy, especially during periods of market turbulence. Unlike stocks, which can exhibit high volatility, bonds generally offer more stable returns and are less susceptible to market fluctuations. This stability can serve as a buffer against the unpredictability of the stock market, making fixed income instruments an essential component for investors seeking to protect their portfolios from potential losses.

One of the primary advantages of incorporating bonds into an investment portfolio is their ability to provide consistent income. Bonds typically pay interest at regular intervals, which can be a reliable source of cash flow. This income can be particularly valuable during times of economic uncertainty when stock dividends may be reduced or eliminated. By focusing on fixed income securities, investors can ensure they have a steady stream of income to rely on, which can help mitigate the financial impact of stock market downturns.

Furthermore, bonds can serve as a diversifying element in an investment portfolio. When equity markets decline, bond prices often behave inversely, meaning that they may appreciate when stocks fall. This inverse relationship can help stabilize a portfolio's overall value, reducing the risk associated with concentrated equity investments. By strategically allocating a portion of their capital to bonds, investors can create a more balanced approach that enhances their resilience during periods of market turbulence.

Investors must also consider the various types of bonds available in the market, each with its own risk and return profile. Government bonds, such as U.S. Treasuries, are generally viewed as low-risk investments, while corporate bonds may offer higher yields at the expense of increased risk. Municipal bonds, another category, can provide tax advantages for investors in higher tax brackets. Understanding these differences allows investors to choose bonds that align with their risk tolerance and investment objectives, further safeguarding their portfolios against market volatility.

In conclusion, the role of bonds and fixed income investments cannot be overstated in the context of navigating market turbulence. By providing stable income, diversification, and varying risk profiles, these investments serve as a vital tool for investors aiming to protect themselves from stock market losses. As market conditions continue to fluctuate, incorporating bonds into an investment strategy can enhance overall financial stability and help investors achieve their long-term financial goals.

Utilizing Hedging Techniques

Hedging techniques serve as essential tools for investors aiming to mitigate risks associated with market volatility. By employing various financial instruments and strategies, investors can protect their portfolios from potential losses caused by adverse market movements. The primary goal of hedging is not to eliminate risk entirely, but to reduce the impact of unfavorable price fluctuations on an investment's value. Understanding these techniques is crucial for anyone looking to master market risk and enhance their investment strategies.

One common hedging method involves the use of options contracts. Options provide the right, but not the obligation, to buy or sell an underlying asset at a predetermined price within a specified timeframe. Investors can utilize put options to safeguard against declines in stock prices. For instance, purchasing a put option allows an investor to sell shares at a set price, effectively establishing a floor for potential losses. This strategy is particularly useful in volatile markets or when an investor anticipates short-term downturns in specific securities.

Another popular hedging technique is the implementation of futures contracts. Futures allow investors to agree to buy or sell an asset at a future date for a predetermined price, which can help lock in profits or protect against losses. This method is frequently used in commodities markets but can also apply to equities and indices. By entering into a futures contract, investors can hedge against adverse price movements by ensuring that they can sell an asset at a specific price, regardless of market conditions at the contract's expiration.

Diversification also plays a vital role in hedging against market risk. By spreading investments across various asset classes, sectors, or geographic regions, investors can reduce their exposure to any single investment's risks. A well-diversified portfolio can help buffer against downturns in specific markets, as losses in one area may be offset by gains in another. This strategy emphasizes the importance of asset allocation and understanding the correlation between different investments to optimize risk management.

Finally, investors can also consider using inverse exchange-traded funds (ETFs) as a hedging strategy. Inverse ETFs are designed to move in the opposite direction of a specific index or asset class. By incorporating these funds into a portfolio, investors can gain protection during market downturns. While inverse ETFs can be effective in hedging, they are also subject to unique risks and complexities, making it essential for investors to conduct thorough research and understand their mechanics before integrating them into their investment strategies. By utilizing these hedging techniques, investors can better navigate market turbulence and protect their investments from significant losses.

Chapter 5: Timing the Market: Is It Possible?

The Myths of Market Timing

The concept of market timing is often surrounded by a cloud of myths that can mislead investors into making poor decisions. One prevalent myth is that experienced investors can consistently predict market movements and capitalize on them. While some may point to individual successes, research shows that even the most seasoned professionals struggle to time the market effectively. This inconsistency is primarily due to the unpredictable nature of markets, which are influenced by a myriad of factors, including economic indicators, geopolitical events, and investor psychology. Relying on the belief that market timing can yield consistent returns can lead to significant financial losses.

Another common myth is the belief that certain indicators or signals can reliably predict market downturns or upswings. Investors often fall into the trap of following trends or relying on popular indicators, such as moving averages or market sentiment. However, these tools can provide misleading signals, especially when used in isolation. Markets are complex systems where numerous variables interact, and relying solely on a specific indicator can result in missed opportunities or ill-timed exits. Understanding that no single indicator can guarantee success is crucial for developing a sound investment strategy.

The myth of the "perfect time to buy" also persists among retail investors. Many believe that waiting for the ideal moment to enter the market will lead to greater profits. This mindset can cause individuals to miss out on significant growth, as markets can change rapidly and unpredictably. Historical data shows that some of the best days in the market often follow the worst ones. By attempting to time these fluctuations, investors may inadvertently lock themselves out of potential gains. A more effective strategy involves a disciplined approach to investing, focusing on long-term goals rather than short-term market movements.

Additionally, the myth that one can avoid losses entirely through market timing can lead to a false sense of security. Many investors attempt to sell off their holdings before a downturn or buy back in at a lower price, believing they can minimize their exposure to risk. However, this approach often leads to emotional decision-making and increased stress. Research indicates that investors who engage in market timing frequently underperform compared to those who adopt a buy-and-hold strategy. The unpredictability of market behavior makes it nearly impossible to avoid losses entirely, emphasizing the importance of risk management and diversification.

Ultimately, recognizing these myths surrounding market timing is essential for navigating market turbulence effectively. Investors should focus on building a robust strategy that prioritizes long-term growth and risk management rather than attempting to predict market movements. Education and awareness of these misconceptions can empower investors to make informed decisions, reducing the likelihood of costly mistakes. By shifting the focus from timing the market to understanding market fundamentals and maintaining a disciplined investment approach, individuals can better protect their investments and achieve their financial goals.

Techniques for Evaluating Market Conditions

Evaluating market conditions is essential for investors looking to safeguard their assets during periods of turbulence. One effective technique is fundamental analysis, which involves examining a company's financial health, industry position, and economic environment. Investors analyze key financial statements, including the balance sheet, income statement, and cash flow statement. By assessing metrics such as earnings per share, price-to-earnings ratios, and debt-to-equity ratios, investors can gauge the intrinsic value of a stock. Understanding these fundamentals helps identify whether a stock is undervalued or overvalued, assisting in making informed investment decisions.

Another technique utilized to evaluate market conditions is technical analysis. This approach focuses on historical price movements and trading volumes to predict future price trends. Investors use various charting tools and indicators, such as moving averages, relative strength index (RSI), and Bollinger Bands, to identify patterns and trends. By analyzing these data points, investors can determine potential entry and exit points for trades. Technical analysis is particularly useful during volatile market conditions, as it helps investors react swiftly to price changes and market sentiment.

Sentiment analysis is also a significant technique for evaluating market conditions. This method involves understanding the overall mood of investors and market participants. Various tools, including surveys, social media sentiment, and news sentiment analysis, can provide insights into how investors are feeling about the market. For example, a high level of fear might indicate that a market downturn is imminent, while growing optimism could signal potential upward momentum. By gauging sentiment, investors can adjust their strategies accordingly, positioning themselves to capitalize on emerging trends or to protect against potential downturns.

Macroeconomic indicators serve as another vital technique for evaluating market conditions. Key indicators, such as gross domestic product (GDP), unemployment rates, inflation rates, and consumer confidence indices, provide insights into the broader economic landscape. Investors monitor these indicators to assess economic health and predict potential market shifts. For instance, rising inflation may lead to tighter monetary policy, impacting interest rates and ultimately affecting stock prices. Understanding these indicators allows investors to anticipate market movements and make strategic adjustments to their portfolios.

Finally, diversification remains a fundamental technique for evaluating and managing market conditions. By spreading investments across various asset classes, sectors, and geographical regions, investors can mitigate risks associated with market volatility. A well-diversified portfolio can weather downturns in specific sectors while benefiting from growth in others. Regularly reviewing and rebalancing the portfolio in response to changing market conditions ensures that investors maintain their desired risk exposure. This proactive approach allows for better resilience against market turbulence, ultimately protecting investments from significant losses.

When to Hold and When to Sell

Understanding when to hold and when to sell investments is crucial for managing market risk effectively. The decision-making process can be influenced by various factors, including market conditions, individual financial goals, and the performance of specific assets. Investors must develop a strategy to evaluate these elements continuously, ensuring that their actions align with their long-term objectives. The ability to discern the right moments to hold or sell can significantly impact an investor's ability to mitigate losses and capitalize on market opportunities.

Holding onto investments during market turbulence can be beneficial if the underlying fundamentals of those assets remain strong. For instance, if a company has solid earnings potential, a strong balance sheet, and a competitive advantage, short-term volatility should not necessarily trigger a sell-off. Instead, investors might consider holding their positions, particularly if they believe the market will recover. This approach requires patience and a thorough understanding of the investment's long-term value, emphasizing the importance of conducting comprehensive research and maintaining a disciplined investment philosophy.

Conversely, there are situations where selling becomes imperative. If an investment's fundamentals deteriorate, such as declining revenues, increasing debt, or negative industry trends, it may be time to reassess the position. Additionally, external factors, such as economic downturns or changes in government policy, can also warrant a reevaluation. Recognizing the signs that an investment may be underperforming or no longer aligns with one's investment strategy is essential. Making timely decisions based on these indicators can help minimize losses and reallocate capital toward more promising opportunities.

Emotional responses can heavily influence the decision to hold or sell, often leading to impulsive choices that do not serve long-term objectives. Investors should strive to maintain a rational perspective, relying on data and analysis rather than succumbing to fear or greed. Developing a disciplined approach that incorporates predefined criteria for both holding and selling can mitigate emotional decision-making. This might include setting target prices, establishing stop-loss orders, or regularly reviewing portfolio performance against market benchmarks.

Ultimately, mastering the art of knowing when to hold and when to sell is a dynamic process that requires ongoing education and adaptability. Investors should remain informed about market trends, economic indicators, and industry developments that could affect their portfolios. By cultivating a proactive mindset and being willing to adjust their strategies in response to changing conditions, investors can enhance their ability to navigate market turbulence effectively, protect their investments, and achieve their financial goals.

Chapter 6: Behavioral Finance and Investor Psychology

Understanding Emotional Decision-Making

Emotional decision-making plays a pivotal role in the financial markets, significantly influencing investor behavior and market outcomes. When individuals encounter market fluctuations, their emotions often drive their responses, leading to decisions that may not align with rational financial strategies. Understanding the psychology behind these emotional responses is essential for anyone seeking to master market risk and avoid losses. Recognizing how fear and greed can cloud judgment allows investors to develop strategies that mitigate emotional influences and promote more disciplined decision-making.

Fear is a predominant emotion that arises during market downturns. Investors may panic when they perceive losses, leading to hasty sell-offs that exacerbate market declines. This fear-driven behavior can result in significant financial setbacks, as decisions made in haste often overlook the fundamentals of investments. By understanding the psychological underpinnings of fear, investors can cultivate a mindset that encourages patience and a long-term perspective. Strategies such as setting predetermined exit points or employing stop-loss orders can help manage fear and provide a structured approach to handling market volatility.

Conversely, greed often manifests during market upswings, tempting investors to chase after quick gains without fully assessing the risks involved. This emotion can lead to overconfidence, prompting investors to overlook critical indicators or dismiss sound analytical practices. Recognizing the allure of greed is crucial for maintaining a balanced investment strategy. Creating a diversified portfolio and adhering to a disciplined investment plan can help mitigate the effects of greed, ensuring that decisions are based on rigorous analysis rather than emotional impulses.

The impact of social influences on emotional decision-making cannot be understated. Investors are often swayed by the narratives surrounding market trends, which can lead to herd behavior. When individuals observe others making profitable trades or reacting to market news, they may feel compelled to follow suit, regardless of their own research or risk tolerance. Awareness of this tendency to conform can empower investors to remain true to their strategic approach. Cultivating a robust understanding of personal investment goals and maintaining a commitment to a well-defined investment strategy are essential in resisting the pull of social pressure.

Ultimately, mastering emotional decision-making is a critical component of navigating market turbulence. By acknowledging and understanding the emotions that drive investment decisions, individuals can take proactive steps to mitigate their impact. Developing emotional intelligence, coupled with strategic planning and disciplined execution, equips investors with the tools necessary to endure the inevitable ups and downs of the market. This approach not only protects investments but also fosters a more resilient mindset that is essential for long-term success in the financial landscape.

Common Psychological Traps

Common psychological traps can significantly impact investment decisions, leading to suboptimal outcomes and increased risk. One prevalent trap is the illusion of control, where investors believe they have more influence over market outcomes than they actually do. This often manifests in overconfidence, as individuals may ignore prevailing market data or trends, believing their unique insight grants them an edge. Such a mindset can lead to excessive trading or holding onto losing investments in the hope of a turnaround, rather than making rational, data-driven decisions.

Another significant psychological trap is loss aversion, a concept rooted in behavioral economics. Investors tend to feel the pain of losses more intensely than the pleasure of equivalent gains. This can result in an irrational reluctance to sell underperforming assets, as individuals may fixate on the potential loss rather than the opportunity to reinvest in more promising options. This tendency can trap investors in a cycle of underperformance, as they cling to losing positions while missing out on better investment opportunities.

Confirmation bias is also a common trap that can distort judgment. Investors often seek information that supports their pre-existing beliefs and ignore data that contradicts them. This selective exposure reinforces their views and can lead to poor investment choices. For instance, an investor convinced that a particular stock is undervalued may disregard negative news or analysis, leading to an inflated sense of security and potentially significant losses when the market corrects.

Anchoring is another psychological trap that investors frequently fall into. This occurs when individuals fixate on a specific reference point, such as a stock's historical price, and use it as the basis for future decisions. For example, if an investor bought a stock at a high price, they may irrationally hold onto it, hoping it will return to that level, rather than assessing its current value or market conditions. This can prevent them from making objective decisions based on the present situation and affect their overall portfolio performance.

Finally, the herd mentality can exacerbate market volatility and lead to irrational decision-making. Investors often feel compelled to follow the actions of others, particularly during periods of market euphoria or panic. This behavior can result in buying high and selling low, as individuals rush to capitalize on perceived trends without conducting thorough analysis. Understanding these psychological traps is crucial for investors aiming to navigate market turbulence effectively, as awareness can empower them to make more rational, informed decisions that align with their investment strategies.

Strategies to Combat Emotional Investing

Emotional investing often leads to poor decision-making, resulting in significant financial losses. To combat this, investors must first recognize and acknowledge their emotions. Understanding the psychological triggers that lead to impulsive buying or selling can help investors develop strategies to manage these feelings. Keeping a journal of emotional responses to market activities can provide insights into patterns that may influence future decisions. By identifying these triggers, investors can take proactive steps to mitigate their impact on investment choices.

Developing a disciplined investment strategy is another effective approach to counter emotional investing. Establishing clear investment goals and a well-defined plan allows investors to maintain focus during market fluctuations. A diversified portfolio tailored to individual risk tolerance can reduce the anxiety associated with market volatility. Regularly reviewing and adjusting the investment strategy, rather than reacting impulsively to market changes, can help keep emotions in check and maintain a long-term perspective.

Utilizing technology can also play a significant role in combating emotional investing. Various tools and platforms offer analytics and data-driven insights that can help investors make informed decisions based on objective criteria rather than emotional impulses. Automated trading systems can execute trades based on pre-set conditions, removing the emotional element from the process. By relying on technology, investors can focus on strategy rather than being swayed by market sentiment.

Engaging with a financial advisor or a support network can further assist in managing emotional investing. Professional guidance can provide an objective perspective, helping investors to remain grounded during turbulent times. Support groups or forums with like-minded investors can also foster a sense of community, encouraging accountability and rational discussions about market conditions. Sharing experiences and insights can help investors navigate their emotional responses more effectively.

Finally, practicing mindfulness and self-care can significantly enhance an investor's ability to manage emotions. Techniques such as meditation, exercise, and stress management can improve overall well-being and clarity of thought. By cultivating a mindful approach to investing, individuals can develop the resilience needed to navigate market turbulence without falling prey to emotional decision-making. Prioritizing mental health and emotional stability is crucial for maintaining a sound investment strategy in the face of market challenges.

Chapter 7: Utilizing Technology and Tools

Investment Platforms and Resources

Investment platforms and resources play a crucial role in helping investors navigate the complexities of the financial markets, particularly during periods of turbulence. As market conditions shift, having access to reliable tools and information can make the difference between protecting your investments and experiencing significant losses. Various online platforms provide comprehensive services, ranging from trading capabilities to educational resources, enabling investors to make informed decisions.

One of the primary types of investment platforms is brokerage firms, which facilitate the buying and selling of securities. These firms offer diverse features, including research reports, real-time data, and analysis tools that are essential for understanding market trends. Many brokerages also provide advanced charting software, allowing investors to perform technical analysis and identify potential entry and exit points for their trades. Selecting a brokerage that aligns with specific investment goals and risk tolerance is critical for successful navigation through market volatility.

In addition to brokerage services, investment research platforms offer invaluable insights into market dynamics. These platforms aggregate data from various sources, providing investors with access to expert analyses, economic indicators, and sector performance metrics. Utilizing these resources can help investors identify patterns and potential risks associated with specific investments.
Furthermore, many platforms include forums or community features where investors can engage with peers, share strategies, and gain perspectives that enhance their understanding of market conditions.

Educational resources are another vital component of mastering market risk. Numerous online courses, webinars, and tutorials are available that cover a wide range of investment topics, from basic principles to advanced strategies. Investors can benefit from learning about risk management techniques, portfolio diversification, and the psychological aspects of trading. By leveraging these educational tools, individuals can build a solid foundation of knowledge that empowers them to make sound investment decisions, particularly in turbulent times.

Finally, staying updated with financial news and market reports is essential for any investor looking to minimize risk. Subscription-based services and financial news websites provide timely updates on economic developments, corporate earnings announcements, and geopolitical events that can impact market conditions. By being informed about these factors, investors can adjust their strategies accordingly and take proactive measures to safeguard their portfolios. Integrating various investment platforms and resources into a cohesive strategy is key to successfully navigating market turbulence and protecting investments from potential losses.

Data Analytics for Informed Decisions

Data analytics has emerged as a pivotal tool in the realm of investment decision-making, particularly in navigating the complexities of market turbulence. By leveraging vast amounts of data, investors can uncover trends and patterns that may not be immediately visible through traditional analysis methods. This approach allows for a more nuanced understanding of market dynamics, enabling informed decisions that align with strategic investment goals. The integration of data analytics into investment strategies not only enhances the ability to predict market movements but also aids in identifying potential risks and opportunities.

One of the primary benefits of data analytics is its capacity to sift through large datasets to extract relevant insights. Investors can utilize advanced algorithms and machine learning techniques to analyze historical market data, economic indicators, and even social media sentiment. By examining these variables, investors can construct a clearer picture of market behavior, which aids in the development of predictive models. These models can be instrumental in forecasting potential downturns or upswings, allowing investors to adjust their portfolios proactively.

Moreover, data analytics facilitates real-time monitoring of market conditions. Investors equipped with analytics tools can track fluctuations in market prices, trading volumes, and emerging trends as they occur. This immediacy allows for timely responses to market shifts, which is crucial in mitigating losses during times of volatility. By staying informed about current market conditions, investors can make decisions based on the latest data rather than relying solely on outdated information or gut feelings.

In addition to enhancing decision-making processes, data analytics also supports risk management strategies. By identifying correlations between different assets and market variables, investors can assess their exposure to various risks. With this understanding, they can implement diversification strategies or hedge against potential losses more effectively. The ability to quantify and model risk through data analytics empowers investors to build robust portfolios that can withstand market fluctuations while achieving their financial objectives.

Finally, the application of data analytics in investment strategies fosters a culture of continuous improvement. As investors gather more data and refine their analytical techniques, they can revisit and adjust their strategies based on performance metrics. This iterative process not only enhances individual investment decisions but also contributes to a more resilient investment approach overall. In the face of market turbulence, embracing data analytics can be the difference between surviving and thriving, providing investors with the insights needed to navigate uncertainty with confidence.

The Impact of Artificial Intelligence on Investing

The integration of artificial intelligence (AI) into the investment landscape has fundamentally altered how investors analyze data and make decisions. Traditionally, investment strategies relied heavily on human intuition and experience, but the advent of AI technologies has introduced a new level of sophistication. Machine learning algorithms can process vast amounts of historical market data, identify patterns, and generate predictive models with remarkable precision. This capability allows investors to uncover insights that may not be apparent through conventional analysis, enhancing their ability to navigate market turbulence effectively.

AI's impact on investing extends beyond data analysis; it also influences trading strategies. High-frequency trading firms leverage AI to execute trades at lightning speed, capitalizing on even the slightest price discrepancies. These algorithms can react to market movements within milliseconds, creating a competitive edge that human traders cannot match. As a result, the market dynamics have shifted, with AI-driven trades contributing to increased volatility. For individual investors, understanding this environment is crucial, as it necessitates a reevaluation of traditional strategies and an adaptation to the new speed of trading.

Risk management is another area where AI is making significant strides. Advanced algorithms can assess risk factors in real time, allowing investors to make informed decisions about their portfolios. By analyzing market trends, economic indicators, and even social media sentiment, AI systems can provide personalized risk assessments tailored to individual investment goals. This proactive approach to risk management empowers investors to adjust their strategies quickly, mitigating potential losses and enhancing overall portfolio resilience during turbulent market conditions.

Moreover, AI enhances the ability to diversify investment portfolios. By utilizing robo-advisors and AI-driven financial platforms, investors can access a broader range of asset classes and investment opportunities. These platforms utilize algorithms to recommend optimal portfolio allocations based on individual risk tolerance and market conditions. As a result, investors can construct well-diversified portfolios that align with their financial objectives while minimizing exposure to specific market risks. This shift towards algorithm-driven diversification is particularly beneficial in volatile markets, where traditional asset allocation strategies may fall short.

While the benefits of AI in investing are significant, it is essential to acknowledge the challenges and risks associated with its implementation. Over-reliance on algorithms can lead to systemic risks, particularly if many investors follow similar AI-driven strategies. Additionally, the lack of transparency in some AI models raises concerns about accountability and trust. As investors increasingly incorporate AI into their decision-making processes, it is crucial to strike a balance between leveraging technology and maintaining a critical perspective on its limitations. Ultimately, understanding the impact of AI on investing equips investors with the knowledge to navigate market turbulence more effectively and protect their investments against potential losses.

Chapter 8: Building a Resilient Investment Portfolio

Characteristics of a Resilient Portfolio

A resilient portfolio is characterized by its ability to withstand market fluctuations while maintaining its long-term growth potential. One of the primary features of such a portfolio is diversification. By spreading investments across various asset classes, sectors, and geographic regions, an investor can mitigate the impact of poor performance in any single area. This strategy reduces volatility and enhances the likelihood of achieving more stable returns over time. A well-diversified portfolio not only includes stocks and bonds but may also integrate real estate, commodities, and alternative investments, each contributing differently to overall risk and return.

Another important characteristic of a resilient portfolio is its alignment with the investor's risk tolerance and investment objectives. Understanding personal risk appetite is crucial in constructing a portfolio that can endure market downturns without triggering panic reactions. A resilient portfolio is tailored to match an individual's financial goals, time horizon, and comfort with market fluctuations. This alignment ensures that when markets become turbulent, the investor is less likely to make impulsive decisions that could jeopardize their long-term objectives.

Liquidity is also a defining trait of a resilient portfolio. Maintaining a portion of liquid assets enables investors to respond swiftly to market changes or personal financial needs without having to sell investments at an inopportune time. This liquidity provides a buffer during market downturns, allowing investors to ride out volatility without being forced to realize losses. A resilient portfolio often includes cash or cash-equivalents, which can serve as a safety net, ensuring that the investor can maintain their strategy even when faced with sudden financial demands.

The incorporation of defensive investments is another hallmark of a resilient portfolio. Defensive stocks, such as those in the utility or consumer staples sectors, tend to perform better during economic downturns. By including these types of investments, a portfolio can provide stability and minimize losses when market conditions are unfavorable. Additionally, fixed-income securities can offer a steady stream of income and lower overall portfolio volatility, further enhancing resilience against market shocks.

Finally, a disciplined rebalancing strategy is crucial for maintaining a resilient portfolio. Over time, market movements can cause an investor's asset allocation to drift away from their original intentions. Regularly reviewing and rebalancing the portfolio ensures that it remains aligned with the investor's goals and risk tolerance. This practice not only helps in capturing gains from outperforming assets but also reinforces the importance of sticking to a long-term strategy, preventing emotional decision-making during periods of market turbulence. By adhering to these characteristics, investors can build portfolios that are better equipped to navigate the complexities and uncertainties of the financial markets.

Regular Portfolio Review and Rebalancing

Regular portfolio review and rebalancing are critical components of effective investment management, particularly in the face of market volatility. As market conditions change, so too can the risk and return profile of an investment portfolio. A well-structured review process allows investors to assess whether their portfolio aligns with their financial goals, risk tolerance, and market outlook. By regularly evaluating the performance of individual assets and the overall portfolio, investors can make informed decisions about necessary adjustments to maximize returns while minimizing risk.

The purpose of rebalancing is to maintain an investor's desired level of asset allocation. Over time, certain assets may perform better than others, leading to an imbalance in the portfolio. For example, if stocks significantly outperform bonds, the portfolio may become overly weighted in equities, increasing its risk exposure. Regular rebalancing involves selling off some of the outperforming assets and reallocating those funds to underperforming or less volatile assets. This process not only helps in maintaining the intended risk profile but also encourages a disciplined approach to investing by enforcing a buy-low, sell-high strategy.

Timing is a crucial factor in portfolio review and rebalancing. While some investors may prefer a periodic review, such as annually or semi-annually, others might adopt a more dynamic approach based on market conditions or specific triggers. For instance, significant market movements or changes in an investor's financial situation may warrant an immediate review. However, frequent trading can lead to higher transaction costs and tax implications, making it essential to strike a balance between responsiveness and cost-effectiveness.

Additionally, a comprehensive portfolio review should include an evaluation of investment performance against benchmarks and a reassessment of investment objectives. Investors should consider whether their financial goals have changed or if their risk tolerance has shifted due to life events, such as changes in income, family circumstances, or retirement plans. By aligning the portfolio with current goals and market realities, investors can better position themselves to navigate potential market turbulence.

Ultimately, regular portfolio review and rebalancing are not merely reactive strategies; they are proactive measures that empower investors to take control of their investment journey. By committing to a systematic review process, investors can enhance their ability to weather market fluctuations and make informed decisions that reflect their financial aspirations. This disciplined approach fosters a long-term perspective, crucial for achieving sustained investment success while mitigating the risks inherent in market volatility.

Adapting to Changing Market Conditions

Adapting to changing market conditions is a critical strategy for investors looking to safeguard their portfolios and maximize returns. The financial landscape is characterized by volatility, driven by factors such as economic shifts, political events, and technological advancements. Investors must remain vigilant and responsive to these changes to minimize risks and seize new opportunities. Understanding the nature of market fluctuations is the first step in developing a robust adaptation strategy.

One effective approach to adapting to changing market conditions is diversification. By spreading investments across various asset classes, sectors, and geographical regions, investors can reduce their exposure to any single market event. During periods of economic uncertainty, certain sectors may outperform while others may lag, making it essential to have a well-rounded portfolio. This strategy not only mitigates potential losses but also positions investors to capitalize on growth in different areas as conditions evolve.

Another key element in adapting to market changes is staying informed about macroeconomic indicators and trends. Regularly monitoring economic data such as GDP growth, unemployment rates, and inflation can provide valuable insights into market direction. Additionally, understanding the impact of fiscal and monetary policies can help investors anticipate changes in market sentiment. Staying informed allows investors to make timely decisions, adjusting their portfolios as necessary to align with emerging conditions.

Technological advancements also play a significant role in how investors adapt to market changes. The rise of algorithmic trading and data analytics enables investors to analyze vast amounts of information rapidly and make informed decisions. Tools such as real-time market tracking apps and artificial intelligence-driven investment platforms can help identify trends and potential risks. Embracing technology can enhance an investor's ability to react swiftly to market shifts, ensuring they remain competitive in a fast-paced environment.

Lastly, cultivating a mindset of flexibility is crucial for adapting to changing market conditions. Investors must be willing to reassess their strategies and make adjustments based on new information and evolving market dynamics. This may involve rebalancing portfolios, exploring alternative investments, or even shifting investment philosophies. A proactive approach to adaptation not only protects investments during turbulent times but also positions investors to take advantage of new opportunities that arise as markets change.

Chapter 9: Case Studies of Successful Investors

Lessons from Warren Buffett

Warren Buffett, often regarded as one of the most successful investors of all time, offers invaluable lessons for those looking to navigate market turbulence. His investment philosophy is rooted in fundamental analysis, patience, and a long-term perspective. One of the core principles Buffett emphasizes is the importance of understanding the intrinsic value of a company. Investors are encouraged to conduct thorough research, analyzing financial statements and market conditions to determine whether a stock is undervalued or overvalued. By focusing on companies with strong fundamentals, investors can mitigate risks and make informed decisions even during volatile market periods.

Another key lesson from Buffett is the significance of a margin of safety. This concept involves buying stocks at a price significantly lower than their calculated intrinsic value, providing a cushion against unforeseen market fluctuations. By ensuring that there is a substantial margin of safety, investors can protect themselves from potential losses. Buffett's approach underscores the necessity of being disciplined and not succumbing to market euphoria or panic, which can lead to poor investment choices. This principle serves as a reminder to remain rational and objective, particularly in turbulent times.

Buffett also advocates for the power of compounding, which he refers to as the "eighth wonder of the world." The concept of compounding highlights the importance of reinvesting earnings to generate additional returns over time. Investors who adopt a long-term outlook can benefit significantly from this strategy, as the effects of compounding can lead to exponential growth of their investments. By focusing on quality companies with strong growth potential and allowing time for their investments to mature, investors can weather market volatility and potentially achieve substantial returns.

Additionally, Buffett teaches the value of emotional resilience in investing. The stock market often experiences cycles of fear and greed, which can lead to irrational behavior among investors. Buffett's calm demeanor and steadfast commitment to his investment principles serve as a model for those looking to maintain their composure during turbulent times. By cultivating emotional discipline and avoiding impulsive reactions to market fluctuations, investors can make more rational decisions that align with their long-term financial goals.

Finally, Buffett's philosophy emphasizes the importance of continuous learning and adaptation. The financial landscape is constantly evolving, and successful investors must stay informed about market trends, economic indicators, and emerging industries. Buffett himself is known for his voracious reading habits and commitment to lifelong learning. By staying educated and open to new ideas, investors can better navigate market turbulence and adjust their strategies to protect their investments. This proactive approach not only enhances investment acumen but also fosters resilience in the face of uncertainty.

Strategies of Peter Lynch

Peter Lynch, renowned for his management of the Fidelity Magellan Fund, developed a series of strategies that have influenced countless investors. His approach emphasizes understanding the companies behind the stocks, advocating for a thorough examination of business fundamentals rather than simply following market trends. Lynch believed that investors should leverage their own knowledge and experiences to identify promising investment opportunities. By focusing on sectors they are familiar with, investors can gain insights that may not be immediately apparent to others in the market.

One of Lynch's key strategies is the concept of "buy what you know." This principle suggests that investors should start with industries or companies they understand. By utilizing personal experiences and insights, they can make informed decisions about potential investments. This strategy not only reduces the risk associated with the investment but also helps in identifying undervalued stocks that may be overlooked by institutional investors. Lynch's success with this approach demonstrates how individual investors can capitalize on their unique perspectives to navigate market turbulence effectively.

Lynch also emphasized the importance of thorough research. He advocated for investors to delve deep into a company's financial statements, management quality, and competitive position. This comprehensive analysis allows investors to evaluate the sustainability of a company's growth. By understanding the underlying factors driving a company's performance, investors can make more rational investment decisions, which is especially crucial during volatile market conditions. Lynch's meticulous attention to detail serves as a reminder that informed investing is a powerful tool in mitigating market risk.

Another critical aspect of Lynch's strategy is the concept of long-term investing. He believed that holding onto quality stocks for an extended period could yield significant returns despite short-term market fluctuations. This long-term perspective encourages investors to remain patient and not react impulsively to daily market movements. By focusing on the fundamentals and ignoring the noise, investors can better position themselves to weather market storms and take advantage of opportunities when they arise.

Finally, Lynch's approach highlights the importance of diversification. While he advocated for concentrating investments in a few well-researched stocks, he also recognized the need for a balanced portfolio to spread risk. By diversifying across different sectors and industries, investors can protect themselves against unforeseen market downturns. This strategy encourages a proactive stance in managing investment risk, allowing investors to navigate turbulent markets with a well-rounded and informed approach. Lynch's strategies not only provide a framework for successful investing but also serve as a guide for managing risk in an unpredictable market environment.

Insights from Ray Dalio

Ray Dalio, the founder of Bridgewater Associates and a prominent figure in the investment world, offers valuable insights that resonate with investors navigating the complexities of market turbulence. His principles, rooted in a deep understanding of economic cycles and market behavior, provide a framework for making informed decisions during volatile periods. Dalio emphasizes the importance of understanding the macroeconomic environment, advocating for a holistic approach that considers various factors influencing market dynamics, including monetary policy, fiscal actions, and geopolitical events.

One of Dalio's key concepts is the idea of radical transparency and radical open-mindedness. He encourages investors to embrace a culture of feedback and learning, which can significantly enhance decision-making processes. By fostering an environment where diverse viewpoints are welcomed, investors can mitigate the risks associated with cognitive biases and emotional decision-making. This principle is particularly relevant during market downturns, where fear and uncertainty can cloud judgment. Investors who remain open to new information and differing perspectives are better positioned to adapt their strategies in response to changing market conditions.

Dalio also highlights the importance of diversification as a fundamental principle for risk management. He argues that a well-diversified portfolio can help cushion against losses during market downturns. By spreading investments across various asset classes, sectors, and geographic regions, investors can reduce the impact of any single investment's poor performance. Dalio's approach encourages a balance between risk and reward, underscoring that while diversification does not guarantee profits, it is a critical strategy for protecting capital in turbulent times.

In addition to diversification, Dalio stresses the significance of understanding and anticipating economic cycles. His analysis of historical market patterns reveals that economies go through cycles of expansion and contraction, influenced by factors such as interest rates, inflation, and consumer behavior. By recognizing the stages of these cycles, investors can make more informed decisions about when to enter or exit positions. Dalio's framework allows investors to align their investment strategies with macroeconomic trends, thereby enhancing their ability to navigate market turbulence effectively.

Lastly, Dalio's emphasis on the importance of a disciplined investment approach cannot be overstated. He advocates for a systematic methodology that incorporates both fundamental analysis and risk assessment. This disciplined approach requires investors to establish clear criteria for investment selection and exit strategies based on predetermined metrics. By adhering to a well-defined process, investors can reduce emotional reactions to market fluctuations and maintain a long-term perspective, which is essential for weathering the inevitable ups and downs of the market. Dalio's insights serve as a guide for investors seeking to master market risk and protect their investments in uncertain environments.

Chapter 10: Preparing for Future Market Challenges

Anticipating Economic Shifts

Anticipating economic shifts is a critical component of effective investment strategy, particularly in an environment characterized by volatility and uncertainty. Investors must remain vigilant and informed about various indicators that signal potential changes in the economic landscape. Key economic indicators, including GDP growth rates, unemployment figures, inflation rates, and consumer confidence indexes, provide valuable insights into the health of an economy. By closely monitoring these metrics, investors can identify trends that may suggest impending economic shifts and adjust their strategies accordingly to mitigate risks.

In addition to traditional economic indicators, geopolitical events and policy changes can significantly influence market dynamics. Trade agreements, changes in government leadership, and international conflicts can lead to rapid and unforeseen economic changes. Investors should be aware of how these factors can impact supply chains, consumer behavior, and overall market sentiment. A well-rounded investment strategy includes staying informed about global news and understanding the potential ramifications of political decisions on financial markets.

Technological advancements also play a crucial role in shaping economic shifts. The rise of digital currencies, automation, and artificial intelligence is transforming industries and creating new market opportunities while rendering others obsolete. Investors must adapt to these technological changes by assessing the long-term viability of their investments in light of emerging trends. Understanding which sectors are poised for growth and which may face disruption is essential for maintaining a resilient investment portfolio.

Furthermore, behavioral economics highlights the importance of market psychology in anticipating economic shifts. Investor sentiment can often drive market movements, sometimes leading to irrational behaviors that do not align with fundamental economic indicators. By recognizing patterns in investor behavior, such as herd mentality or panic selling, investors can position themselves to capitalize on opportunities that arise during market corrections. Developing an understanding of the psychological aspects of investing allows for more informed decision-making in turbulent times.

Finally, scenario analysis can be an effective tool for anticipating economic shifts. By exploring various economic scenarios—such as recession, recovery, or inflationary periods—investors can better prepare for potential market movements. Creating contingency plans based on different scenarios enables investors to respond swiftly and effectively to changes in the economic environment. This proactive approach not only helps in protecting investments but also positions investors to seize opportunities that may arise in the wake of economic shifts.

The Role of Global Events in Market Movements

Global events significantly influence market movements, often serving as catalysts for rapid changes in investor sentiment and asset valuations. These events can range from geopolitical tensions and economic policy changes to natural disasters and pandemics. Each of these occurrences can disrupt market stability, leading to volatility that investors must navigate carefully. Understanding the mechanisms through which global events impact markets is crucial for those looking to master market risk and protect their investments.

Geopolitical events, such as conflicts or diplomatic negotiations, can create uncertainty in the financial markets. For instance, military conflicts can lead to increased oil prices, affecting sectors reliant on energy. Investors often react swiftly to news from these regions, causing stock prices to fluctuate dramatically. Monitoring geopolitical developments is essential for investors, as it allows them to anticipate potential market shifts and adjust their strategies accordingly. This vigilance can mitigate risks associated with sudden market downturns driven by external factors.

Economic data releases and policy decisions by central banks also play a vital role in shaping market movements. For example, announcements regarding interest rate changes or inflation reports can trigger immediate reactions in stock and bond prices. Investors must remain informed about economic indicators and the broader macroeconomic environment to gauge potential impacts on their portfolios. A proactive approach to understanding these economic signals can empower investors to make informed decisions and capitalize on opportunities presented by changing market conditions.

Natural disasters and public health crises, such as hurricanes or pandemics, can have profound effects on the global economy. The COVID-19 pandemic, for instance, led to unprecedented market volatility as businesses shut down and consumer behavior shifted dramatically. Investors who were unprepared for such an event faced significant losses. In contrast, those who had strategies in place to respond to crises were better positioned to mitigate risks and even find new avenues for growth. Developing contingency plans for potential global events is essential for safeguarding investments against unforeseen disruptions.

In conclusion, the interplay between global events and market movements underscores the importance of staying informed and adaptable. By recognizing how geopolitical tensions, economic indicators, and unforeseen crises impact financial markets, investors can enhance their ability to navigate turbulence. Mastering market risk requires a comprehensive understanding of these dynamics, enabling investors to protect their assets and seize opportunities amidst uncertainty. Embracing a proactive investment strategy that accounts for global events can significantly improve one's chances of success in the ever-changing landscape of financial markets.

Building Long-Term Investment Strategies

Building long-term investment strategies requires a comprehensive understanding of market dynamics and personal financial goals. Investors must first recognize that successful long-term investing is not merely about selecting the right stocks but involves a systematic approach that includes risk assessment, diversification, and continuous evaluation of one's portfolio. The foundation of any robust investment strategy is the establishment of clear objectives. These objectives should align with the investor's risk tolerance, time horizon, and financial aspirations. A well-defined goal helps in making informed investment decisions and provides a benchmark for evaluating performance.

A critical component of a long-term investment strategy is diversification. This approach helps mitigate risk by spreading investments across various asset classes, sectors, and geographical regions. By diversifying, investors can protect themselves against market volatility, as different assets tend to react differently to economic changes. For instance, while stocks may experience downturns, bonds or real estate might hold their value or even appreciate. An effective diversification strategy involves not only mixing asset classes but also rebalancing the portfolio periodically to maintain the desired allocation and risk level.

Investors must also adopt a disciplined approach to market analysis and research. Staying informed about market trends, economic indicators, and geopolitical events can enhance decision-making processes. Long-term investors should focus on fundamental analysis rather than short-term market fluctuations. This involves examining a company's financial health, industry position, and growth potential. By prioritizing quality investments with strong fundamentals, investors can weather market turbulence more effectively and capitalize on growth opportunities over time.

Emotional discipline plays a significant role in building long-term investment strategies. Market volatility can trigger fear and anxiety, leading to impulsive decisions that may jeopardize investment goals. Developing a mindset focused on long-term objectives rather than short-term gains is essential. Investors should establish a plan that includes predetermined entry and exit points, allowing them to stick to their strategy even during turbulent times. This commitment to a long-term vision can help investors avoid the pitfalls of panic selling and maintain their course through market fluctuations.

Lastly, continuous education and self-assessment are vital for refining investment strategies. The financial landscape is ever-evolving, and staying updated on new investment vehicles, market trends, and economic policies can enhance an investor's ability to navigate challenges. Regularly reviewing and adjusting investment strategies based on performance and changing market conditions ensures that the portfolio remains aligned with the investor's goals. By committing to lifelong learning and adaptability, investors can build resilient long-term investment strategies that withstand market turbulence and contribute to sustained financial success.

Chapter 11: Conclusion: Navigating the Future of Investing

Embracing Change in Investment Strategies

Change is an inevitable part of investing, particularly in volatile markets. Embracing change in investment strategies is essential for investors seeking to protect their portfolios and capitalize on new opportunities. A flexible approach allows investors to adapt to shifting market conditions, economic indicators, and global events. Acknowledging that what worked in the past may no longer be effective is the first step toward developing a robust investment strategy that can withstand market turbulence.

The ability to adapt investment strategies requires continuous monitoring of market trends and economic data. Investors should familiarize themselves with key indicators such as interest rates, inflation, and employment rates, as these factors can significantly influence market performance. By staying informed, investors can make timely adjustments to their portfolios, reallocating resources to sectors that show promise while reducing exposure to those that are underperforming. This proactive approach helps mitigate risk and ensures that investments remain aligned with current market dynamics.

Moreover, diversification remains a cornerstone of effective investment strategy, particularly in times of uncertainty. Investors must be willing to reassess their asset allocations regularly. This might involve shifting funds between equities, fixed income, real estate, and alternative investments. By broadening their investment horizons, investors can better protect themselves against downturns in specific sectors. Embracing change often means seeking out new asset classes or investment vehicles that may not have been considered previously, thus enhancing overall portfolio resilience.

Technology advancements have also transformed the investment landscape, offering new tools for analysis and execution. Investors should embrace these innovations, such as algorithmic trading, robo-advisors, and data analytics platforms. These tools can provide valuable insights into market trends and help investors make informed decisions quickly. By leveraging technology, investors can enhance their ability to respond to market changes swiftly, ensuring that their investment strategies remain relevant and effective.

Finally, an open mindset is crucial when embracing change in investment strategies. This involves being willing to learn from both successes and failures. Investors should regularly review their performance, analyze what strategies were effective, and identify areas for improvement. Engaging with financial professionals, participating in investment seminars, and consuming educational content can provide fresh perspectives and inspire innovative approaches. By fostering a culture of continuous learning, investors can navigate market turbulence with confidence, ensuring their strategies evolve in tandem with the ever-changing investment landscape.

Continuous Learning and Adaptation

Continuous learning and adaptation are essential components for investors looking to navigate the complexities of market turbulence effectively. The financial landscape is constantly evolving due to technological advancements, regulatory changes, and shifting consumer preferences. Investors must cultivate a mindset that embraces lifelong learning to stay ahead of these changes. This involves not only keeping abreast of market trends but also understanding the underlying factors driving these trends. By engaging in continuous education, investors can better position themselves to make informed decisions that protect their portfolios from potential losses.

One effective approach to continuous learning is leveraging a variety of resources, including financial news outlets, academic journals, and investment seminars. Each of these sources offers unique insights and perspectives that can enhance an investor's understanding of market dynamics. For instance, financial news can provide real-time updates on market movements, while academic research may offer in-depth analyses of economic theories and their practical implications. Additionally, attending seminars or workshops can foster networking opportunities with other investors and industry experts, leading to valuable exchanges of ideas and strategies.

Adaptation is equally crucial in the face of market turbulence. Investors must be willing to adjust their strategies in response to new information and shifting market conditions. This might involve reallocating assets, diversifying portfolios, or adopting new investment vehicles. The ability to pivot quickly can significantly mitigate risks associated with volatile markets. For example, an investor who identifies a downturn in a specific sector can proactively shift investments toward more stable industries or explore alternative investment opportunities, such as bonds or commodities, that may offer greater security during turbulent times.

Furthermore, technology plays a pivotal role in facilitating continuous learning and adaptation. Online platforms and trading tools have made it easier for investors to access real-time data and analytics, allowing them to make timely decisions based on current market conditions. Automated trading systems and algorithms can also assist in executing trades based on predefined criteria, reducing the emotional aspects of investing. By embracing technological advancements, investors can enhance their ability to respond swiftly to market changes and optimize their investment strategies.

In conclusion, continuous learning and adaptation are vital for investors who aim to master market risk and protect their investments. By committing to ongoing education and being flexible in their approaches, investors can better navigate the uncertainties of the financial markets. This proactive mindset not only helps in mitigating potential losses but also positions investors to seize opportunities that may arise even in times of turbulence. Embracing this philosophy will empower individuals to develop resilience in their investment strategies, ultimately leading to more sustainable financial success.

Final Thoughts on Market Resilience

Market resilience is a critical concept for investors seeking to navigate the complexities of financial turbulence. It refers to the ability of markets to recover from shocks and maintain their functionality over time. Understanding the characteristics of resilient markets enables investors to develop strategies that not only protect their assets but also capitalize on opportunities that arise during periods of instability. By recognizing the signs of resilience, investors can make informed decisions that align with their long-term financial goals.

One essential aspect of market resilience is the role of diversification. A well-diversified portfolio can withstand the impact of adverse market conditions, as losses in one area may be offset by gains in another. Investors should consider spreading their investments across different asset classes, sectors, and geographical regions to reduce overall risk. This diversification strategy is particularly effective in turbulent times when certain markets or sectors may experience heightened volatility. By employing this approach, investors can create a buffer against market fluctuations while positioning themselves for potential recovery.

Another crucial factor contributing to market resilience is the importance of maintaining a long-term perspective. Short-term market movements can often lead to panic selling or impulsive decisions, which can undermine investment strategies. Instead, investors should focus on their long-term objectives and remain disciplined in their approach. Historical data shows that markets tend to recover from downturns over time, and those who stay the course are often rewarded for their patience. Emphasizing a long-term outlook helps investors navigate through turbulence and minimizes the likelihood of making emotional decisions driven by fear.

In addition to diversification and a long-term perspective, investors must also be aware of the economic indicators that signal market resilience. Metrics such as consumer confidence, employment rates, and corporate earnings can provide valuable insights into the health of the economy and the potential for market recovery. By monitoring these indicators, investors can gauge the overall sentiment and make more informed decisions regarding their investments. Recognizing the signs of resilience in the market can lead to timely adjustments in strategy, allowing investors to take advantage of favorable conditions as they arise.

Ultimately, fostering an understanding of market resilience equips investors with the tools necessary to weather financial storms. By embracing diversification, maintaining a long-term perspective, and staying informed about economic indicators, investors can not only protect their investments but also enhance their potential for growth. As markets continue to evolve and present new challenges, those who prioritize resilience in their investment strategies will likely emerge stronger and more prepared for future market fluctuations.

www.ingramcontent.com/pod-product-compliance
Lightning Source LLC
Chambersburg PA
CBHW070237220526
45465CB00004B/1445